ABOVE
ALL
LIBERTIES

ABOVE ALL LIBERTIES

by
ALEC CRAIG

Essay Index Reprint Series

 BOOKS FOR LIBRARIES PRESS
FREEPORT, NEW YORK

HQ462
C7

First Published 1942
Reprinted 1972

Library of Congress Cataloging in Publication Data

Craig, Alec.
   Above all liberties.

   (Essay index reprint series)
   Reprint of the 1942 ed.
   Bibliography: p.
   1. Obscenity (Law)--Gt. Brit. 2. Literature,
Immoral--History. I. Title.
HQ462.C7   1972   364.17'4   70-37839
ISBN 0-8369-2587-4

PRINTED IN THE UNITED STATES OF AMERICA
BY
NEW WORLD BOOK MANUFACTURING CO., INC.
HALLANDALE, FLORIDA 33009

CONTENTS

CHAPTER		PAGE
	Introduction	9
I.	"MERRY ENGLAND"	13
II.	EDMUND CURLL	25
III.	THE MAKING OF A LAW	36
IV.	HAVELOCK ELLIS	44
V.	THE STRANGE CASE OF COUNT POTOCKI OF MONTALK	75
VI.	THE WIDER CENSORSHIP	97
VII.	*TO BEG I AM ASHAMED*	110
VIII.	CONTRAST WITH U.S.A.	121
IX.	*OUTRAGE AUX MŒURS*	137
X.	THE PROBLEM OF PORNOGRAPHY	163
	Bibliography	191
	Index	197

159813

INTRODUCTION

THE response of the public to my previous work, *The Banned Books of England*, was most gratifying. It demonstrated that numerous thoughtful and educated men and women in all grades of society still hold the freedom of English letters dear. The press is indifferent to all that does not make for a "sensation" or a "story"; politicians are aloof from every cause without vote-catching potentialities; officialdom is cautious and complacent: nevertheless the love of literary freedom is as strong as ever it was in the past. I was rewarded for my humble task with a volume of correspondence, and a series of interesting personal contacts for which I cannot be too grateful. I thus became possessed of an accumulation of new facts and references which would have gone far to perfect and embellish *The Banned Books of England*. The problem was: How to present this new material to the public? There were two objections to the obvious solution of a new and revised edition. In the first place, it would scarcely have been fair to the purchasers of the original edition to supersede it so quickly. In the second place, such a revision would have involved some departure from the rather severe limits which I laid down in writing the book: namely, to give only "an exposition of the present situation sufficiently detailed to equip the reformer with the knowledge necessary for his task,

Above All Liberties

together with so much of past history as is necessary to a proper understanding of the present." The book was essentially one for the reformer.

I resolved therefore to write a new book. I resolved to re-state my case for a rather different class of reader, or more accurately for a wider class of readers. I would address myself to all lovers of literature whether imbued with reforming zeal or not.

In carrying out this task I have repeated scarcely any of the matter contained in the earlier work. Most of the legal argument has gone by board—no great loss, perhaps, in a sphere where the operation of the law is so arbitrary as to render it almost unworthy of being called "law." I have, however, elaborated one new legal point for which I am indebted to Mr. Geoffrey Faber's review in the *Listener* of April 28, 1937, namely, that the famous Cockburn definition of "obscenity" should not rank as law at all. I have adopted an historical method of presentation in which the problem is set against the background of English literary and social changes. I have sought to enhance the interest of my book by dealing in detail with three human personalities who play a part in my story: one, an eighteenth-century rascal; another, one of the few men of our time whom I believe posterity will call Great; and a third who was persecuted, it seems to me, because he is one of the tiny minority who, in any essential way, break the drab uniformity of our modern age. I have dealt with such suppressions,

Introduction

and attempted suppressions, as have occurred in England and America since the publication of the former work. Finally, by adding a chapter on France to studies already covering the United States and the British Empire, I include in my survey practically the whole area in which those ideals of freedom and reason that have inspired my work receive even so much as lip service.

This is the time to express my thanks to various persons who have assisted me in that survey. First of all, I am greatly indebted to the Keeper of the Printed Books, and his officers, at the British Museum. It is an encouraging sign in a gloomy world that a reader with nothing but patience and devotion to recommend him, working in a field dominated by prejudice and passion and considered the special preserve of the fanatic, the fool and the crank, should receive every courtesy and assistance in our great national library. The National Council for Civil Liberties have also been most helpful. In regard to passages on America I am indebted for material supplied by the National Council on Freedom from Censorship, New York, Dr. Norman Himes and Mr. G. E. Legman. Messrs. George Routledge & Sons were good enough to allow me to reproduce their letters to the *New Statesman and Nation*. I thank Mr. A. J. Moore for reading the proofs. Finally, I record my gratitude to Ivy Dey, without whose inspiration and generosity my task would not have been accomplished.

Above All Liberties

It may be objected that this is no time to bring this subject before the public. It may be claimed that however fundamentally important it may be, it is neither urgent nor closely related to our present distresses. I disagree. I have lived to see history repeat itself like a nightmare. If the process continues the time will come when the young people of our own and other nations will again address themselves to the task of reconstructing the ruin made by the folly of their elders. Their task, properly conceived, must embrace the whole of life in a revolutionary reform. In no sphere will their difficulties be greater than in that of sexual ethics. Nowhere will they find obscurantism and clericalism so firmly entrenched, so blatant and so unashamed as in the realm of sexual knowledge. Here the primary necessity of all human progress, intellectual liberty, is denied. In the nature of things, such a situation cannot stand still. It must either improve or deteriorate. To protest in and out of season, is a service to the youth of to-morrow. To them, in the future, and to Havelock Ellis, in the past, I dedicate my book.

A. C.

BRICKET WOOD, HERTS
July 1941

CHAPTER I

"MERRY ENGLAND"

In the Middle Ages it was assumed that what a man believed and what a man thought was the business of the Church. In theory, intellectual speculation and a private life of his own were alike denied him. In practice, the power of princes and of the great nobles protected him to some extent from ecclesiastical interference and under the shadow of their protection humbler men here and there experienced something of freedom. For example, it was the protection of John of Gaunt that enabled Wyclif to die a natural death at Lutterworth: and left the Church to wreak a futile vengeance on his bones. But freedom was the exception, not the rule. The ecclesiastical courts were there to enforce compliance with the will of the Church. In primitive times they relied on admonition and excommunication; but gradually, fines, imprisonment and the stake were added to their sanctions. In this country we have only vestigial remains of this powerful judicial machinery in the courts that try cases of clerical discipline.

When printing was invented in the fifteenth century, the production of books was, as a matter of course, subjected to the closest control. But the new technique proved too much for a religious system

Above All Liberties

which had grown corrupt as it relied more and more on external force, and less and less on inner conviction, to lead men into right action. To-day ecclesiastical censorship survives only in the *Index Librorum Prohibitorum* of the Roman Church, and in the control she exercises over authors who submit to her obedience.

The *Index Librorum Prohibitorum* should not be confused with the *Index Librorum Expurgatorius*, a projected catalogue, never published, of works allowed to be read after the deletion or amendment of specified passages. The *Index Librorum Prohibitorum* consists of a list of some four thousand books forbidden throughout the world and in every translation. No layman may read any of them without special permission granted only for single books and exclusively in urgent cases. The latest edition of the *Index*, published in the Vatican City in 1938, includes some astonishing items: Gibbon's *Decline and Fall of the Roman Empire*, Larousse's *Grand Dictionnaire Universel*, Montaigne's *Essays*, Ranke's *History of the Popes*, Richardson's *Pamela*, Taine's *History of English Literature*. Hugo's *Notre-Dame de Paris* and his *Les Misérables* are also included, while of Balzac, Dumas (*pater et filius*) and George Sand "*omnes fabulae amatoriae*" are condemned. The list also contains works by Hobbes, La Fontaine, Locke, J. S. Mill, Pascal, Stendhal and Voltaire. At one time Boccaccio's *Decameron* was on the list, except for an

"Merry England"

edition published under the auspices of the Council of Trent in 1573 where all the gallantries are retained, but the clerical sinners are metamorphosised into laymen.

As regards authorship, no Roman Catholic, priest or layman, may publish, without previous approval of the Censor, any book on theology, Church history, canon law, ethics, or other religious or moral subject. The effect of this regulation was brought home to Mr. Alfred Noyes, a convert to Roman Catholicism, over his book on Voltaire in 1938. Denounced to the Holy Office by an anonymous informer, the book had to be withdrawn until the author had made his peace with the clerical authorities by writing an explanatory preface dealing with some points of Church history.[1]

If in countries like our own where liberalism has become the very life-blood of our intellectual existence, the full rigour of the Church's law is not always felt by Roman Catholics, it is because living in *partibus infidelium* they enjoy a measure of the freedom hardly won by generations of Protestants and Agnostics. In Catholic countries it is far otherwise. The *Index* and the ecclesiastical censorship are respected by the faithful, and the Church is ever ready to employ the arm of the civil law against writing of which it disapproves. For instance, a summary of H. G. Wells' *The Fate of Homo Sapiens* published in

[1] See correspondence in the *Times* and the *New Statesman and Nation* during August and September 1938.

Above All Liberties

the periodical *Picture Post* contained a strong attack on Roman Catholicism in Eire. There was a vehement outcry from the Catholic press, and the *Irish Catholic* demanded the banning of what it called a "filthy, immoral and suggestive" publication. The editor of *Picture Post* offered the editor of the *Irish Catholic* space in which to reply to Wells in vain. Similar facilities for reply were offered to a Roman Catholic Archbishop and to Hilaire Belloc. The Archbishop pleaded "pressure of work" and Mr. Belloc was willing to supply a review of the book for no less than £50. In the end, *Picture Post* was banned by the Government of Eire for three months under the Censorship of Publications Act, 1929.[1] These things should not surprise us, for the attitude of authority has been declared for all time in the Syllabus of Pius IX issued in 1869:

Whoso shall say that the Roman pontiff can, or ought to, reconcile himself to, or compromise with, liberalism, progress or modern civilisation *anathema sit*.

The Reformation in England gave a blow to the ecclesiastical courts, after which they slowly withered, until in 1876 the desuetude of their jurisdiction over the laity was judicially recognised in *Phillimore* v. *Machin*. For more than a century, however, the claims of the royal prerogative were as tyrannous as ever an ecclesiastical court had been so far as the censorship

[1] See the *Bulletin of the Council for Investigation of Vatican Influence and Censorship* for February 15, 1940.

"Merry England"

of literature was concerned.[1] Henry VIII entrusted the censorship of books to the then recently constituted Court of Star Chamber. In 1585, at Archbishop Whitgift's instigation, the Court passed regulations requiring that no book, with unimportant exceptions, could be printed without being perused and allowed by the Archbishop of Canterbury or Bishop of London. The task of perusal was generally deputed to a chaplain.

The flood of translations from the Italian which was one of the features of the Renaissance in England was particularly deplored by the moralists of the time. There is a familiar ring to modern ears about Roger Ascham's denunciation in his *Schoolmaster*:

> It is a pity that those which have authority and charge, to allow and disallow books to be printed, be no more circumspect herein, than they are. Ten sermons at Paul's cross do not so much good for moving men to true doctrine, as one of those books do harm, with inticing men to ill living. . . . They open, not fond and common ways to vice, but such subtle, cunning, new and diverse shifts, to carry young wills to vanity and young wits to mischief, to teach old bawds new school points, as the simple head of an Englishman is not able to invent, nor never was heard of in England before.

Ascham had particularly in mind Painter's *Palace of Pleasure*, that treasury of story which Shakespeare

---

[1] The history of prerogative control over printing was recently examined in *Attorney-General for New South Wales* v. *Butterworth & Co.* (*The Author*, for Summer, 1940.)

and his contemporary dramatists rifled for their plots; but he was too wily to advertise the book by naming it. The controversial device of defaming an opponent's work without specifying it sufficiently to enable the reader to form an independent judgment by referring to it, is not uncommon among religious writers to-day.

The powers of the bishops over the press were by no means sufficient to satisfy Laud. In 1637 he obtained from the Star Chamber a decree dealing with books imported from abroad. It provided that no packages of books could be imported for sale without a catalogue being first submitted to the Archbishop of Canterbury or the Bishop of London, who, by their agents, were to superintend the unloading of the books.

The Long Parliament abolished the detested Court of Star Chamber, and Milton in his *Areopagitica* exposed and denounced for all time the anomalies, absurdities and tyrannies of literary censorship. After the Restoration, however, an Act was passed making the licence of a press censor necessary before anything could be printed. Furthermore, the Ecclesiastical Courts, abolished in 1640, were reconstituted; but they were less effective than ever and their importance continued to diminish as time went on.

There was much learned argument in Sir Charles Sedley's case as to whether he and his companions should not have been tried before an ecclesiastical

"Merry England"

court, instead of before the Lord Chief Justice. The offence concerned was an outrage on public decency of very disgusting sort; but it is worth a glance not only for its legal interest but for the light it throws on the manners of the time. Social conditions are as much a cause of the state of the law as they are an effect of the operation of law.

Sir Charles Sedley was one of the boon companions of Charles II and a member of the young Circle of Wits of which the Earl of Rochester became another. Besides their activities as courtiers, these young men haunted the taverns of London. There they functioned as the perhaps degenerate heirs of the tradition of Shakespeare, Ben Jonson and the revellers of the Mermaid Tavern. They were, however, instrumental in handing on that tradition, through Addison and Steele, to Johnson and Goldsmith. The taverns in the neighbourhood of Charing Cross were accustomed to witness the most unseemly scenes enacted by these young Restoration blades, but on one occasion all limits were exceeded and the hand of justice fell. Anthony à Wood[1] tells the story in these words. "In the month of June 1663 this our author, Sir Ch. Sedley, Charles Lord Buckhurst (afterwards Earl of Middlesex) Sir Tho. Ogle, etc, were at a cook's house at the sign of the Cock in Bow-street near Covent-garden, within the liberty of Westm. and being inflam'd with strong liquors,

[1] *Athenae Oxonienses* (1813–20), IV, p. 731.

Above All Liberties

they went into the balcony belonging to that house, and putting down their breeches they excrementiz'd in the street: which being done, Sedley stripped himself naked, and with eloquence preached blasphemy to the people: whereupon a riot being raised, the people became very clamorous, and would have forced the door next to the street open: but being hindred, the preacher and his company were pelted into their room, and the windows belonging thereunto were broken. This frolick thing being soon spread abroad, especially by the fanatical party who aggravated it to the utmost, by making it the most scandalous thing in nature, and nothing more reproachful to religion than that; the said company were summoned to the court of justice in Westminster-hall, where being indicted of a riot before Sir Rob. Hyde, lord chief justice of the common pleas, were all fined, and Sir Charles being fined 500l. he made answer, that he thought he was the first man that paid for . . ." and here the gay baronet had the last word, and a word very disrespectful to the Court too!

Sedley, for all his wild ways, was a respectable poet. His only daughter, Katherine, became the mistress of the Duke of York. When the Duke ascended the throne he created her Countess of Dorchester. These circumstances "greatly shocked" the dissolute Sir Charles and put some strain on his loyalty. After the abdication he supported the accession of William and Mary. When someone found this attitude

"Merry England"

strange in an old courtier of Charles II, Sedley answered, "Well, I am even in point of civility with King James. For as he made my daughter a Countess, so I have helped to make his daughter a Queen."

Katherine's influence on her royal lover was good. She worked hard for the Protestant cause, and if anything could have saved James from his fate it would have been her strong understanding, good-nature, and acute sense of humour. When James was no longer King she married a worthy knight to whom she bore two sons. When sending them off to school she is reported to have said: "If anybody call either of you the son of a whore, you must bear it; for you are so: but if they call you bastards, fight till you die; for you are an honest man's sons."

Reminiscences of the seventeenth century are perhaps not altogether edifying, but on the other hand the age produced some of the most exquisite poetry in the English language, as well as the last music that was wholly English in character. To-day madrigal societies sing prudently selected examples and emasculated versions of songs which were then heard up and down the country: while the books of "Drolleries" serve to remind us of a time when England was "merry."

The statute imposing the censorship of the press was allowed to expire in 1695, and nothing like it has been put into force since except for a period during

Above All Liberties

the war of 1914–1918.[1] Books and journals were no longer censored in the true sense of that word, that is, subjected to control before publication. The liberty of the press has become part of the English heritage. This liberty was briefly defined by Lord Mansfield in *R. v. Dean of St. Asaph* in 1784: "The liberty of the press consists in printing without previous licence subject to the consequences of the law."

The law whose consequences may follow publication is the law of libel. Libel may be defamatory, seditious, blasphemous or obscene. Both the criminal and civil courts provide remedies for persons aggrieved by defamation. Sedition is outside the scope of this book. Blasphemous libel is almost a dead letter; but not quite, as the following astonishing case will show:

> On a charge of having published a blasphemous libel, Arthur Reynolds Woodhall, 47, proprietor of the Mayfair Hotel, Jersey, described as a free-lance photographer, was at Jersey Assizes yesterday sentenced to a month's imprisonment.
> Mr. Clifford Orange, Chief Aliens Officer, stated that when Woodhall called at his office at St. Helier to obtain an exit permit his passport contained two photographs, one of which showed Woodhall lying on the beach wearing bathing drawers, and with arms outstretched. Sketched in were a cross and other marks, making the picture what Mr.

---

[1] In 1918 *Despised and Rejected* by A. T. Fitzroy (the pseudonym of Miss Rose Allatini), a novel about a conscientious objector, was suppressed after publication as being prejudicial to recruiting and military discipline. I note that the hero (as also the heroine) is homosexual.

"*Merry England*"

Orange described as a representation of Christ crucified. (*Daily Telegraph*, January 10, 1940.)

This book is concerned with obscene libel, a branch of the law of libel which did not exist in the seventeenth century. This is quite clear from the remarks of Judge Powell in *R.* v. *Read* (1708) where it was unsuccessfully attempted to punish a man for printing a book entitled *The Fifteen Plagues of a Maidenhead*:

"This is for printing bawdy stuff, that reflects on no person," said the judge, "and a libel must be against some particular person or persons, or against the Government. It is stuff not fit to be mentioned publicly. If there is no remedy in the Spiritual court, it does not follow there must be a remedy here. There is no law to punish it: I wish there were: but we cannot make law. It indeed tends to the corruption of good manners, but that is not sufficient for us to punish. As to the case of Sir Charles Sedley, there was something more in that case than showing his naked body in the balcony."

And the judge pointed out that the gravamen of the case was the disgusting assault on the people in the street below.

We have traced the decline of control over literature in relation to sexual matters from a time when such control was taken for granted as a part (though not an important part) of a vast engine of oppression by means of which the Church asserted control over

Above All Liberties

the most intimate thoughts and actions of men. We have come to a point where liberty in this respect is so complete that it is no offence to sell even an admittedly bawdy book.

CHAPTER II

EDMUND CURLL

EDMUND CURLL is chiefly remembered to-day as a figure in Pope's *Dunciad*. Curll was a remarkable man in a remarkable setting. A comparison between the Grub Street of the Augustan age of English literature and the publishing world of to-day should provide encouragement to those lugubrious philosophers who assure us that nothing can improve and that human nature is incorrigible. In the first part of the eighteenth century paid authorship, let alone publishing, was scarcely considered an occupation proper to a gentleman. The law of copyright was in its infancy; and that of defamatory libel, a puny forerunner of its present self. Piracy, spurious title pages, sharp practice, lying, and even fraud were the order of the day. In this literary jungle, Curll was conspicuous as a beast of prey who always knew a trick a little shadier than the tricks of his rivals; whose daring and impudence were regarded with astonishment and, likely enough, with envy; whose bawdiness upset the susceptibilities of a coarse age; and whose treatment of his hack authors outraged the by no means exacting standards of his time. On the other hand, he had taste, ability and a genuine enthusiasm for literature and scholarship;

Above All Liberties

and was treated quite seriously by many reputable men of letters.

This dual character resulted in a lively and troublous existence. Born in 1675 he came to Town in 1705. As early as 1708 he was involved in bitter controversies with rivals over his *Charitable Surgeon*, a quack treatise on venereal disease recommending remedies which, curiously enough, could always be bought in Curll's shop. A little later he entered with gusto into current religious controversy and lent his own pen to champion the superior merits of the Church of England against all comers.

Things became serious when his unauthorised publication of some poems opened his long quarrel with the great Alexander Pope. Incredible as it may sound, Pope won one bout of this conflict by administering an emetic to Curll in the guise of a friendly bottle of wine at the Swan Tavern in Fleet Street. Pope then wrote a lampoon mocking at Curll's sufferings when he returned to the bosom of his family. This was followed by another similar pamphlet, and finally, at a later date, he produced: *A Strange but True Relation how Mr. Edmund Curll out of an Extraordinary Desire of Lucre, went into Change Alley and was converted from the Christian religion by Certain Eminent Jews; and how he was circumcised, and initiated into their Mysteries*. Curll did not take all this lying down, but retorted with squibs which made up in venom for what they lacked in genius.

Edmund Curll

The quarrel with Pope began in 1715, the year of the first Jacobite rising. Curll was to get into further trouble for publishing a cheap edition of the proceedings in the House of Lords against the Earl of Winton, the only one of the impeached peers who did not plead guilty and throw himself on the mercy of George I. The Lords regarded this as a breach of privilege and Curll was reprimanded on his knees by the Lord Chancellor after three weeks' loss of liberty. Curll must have regarded this affair as particularly unfortunate as he had taken the precaution of describing his print as "translated from the French" and of issuing it under the imprint of a woman bookseller who happened to be ill at the time.

A few years after he was again on his knees in the House of Lords. Curll could give points even to modern publishers and authors in the alacrity with which he would produce a biography of a deceased person of eminence. When the first Duke of Buckinghamshire died, sure enough, Curll was first in the field with an announcement of Works, Life and Last Will and Testament of the late peer, all of course unauthorised. The Lords took umbrage, and Curll was again reprimanded although this time he escaped imprisonment.

The House of Lords was not the only institution in Westminster offended by (and able to revenge itself on) our publisher. In 1716 the Captain of Westminster School pronounced a funeral oration in Latin

Above All Liberties

over the body of the famous Dr. Robert South. Curll thought it worth while to print this effusion with an English translation. Perhaps he thought it would prepare the ground for the inevitable "Life." Anyway it was not to be expected that in such a case a man like Curll would worry about authorisation; but he was probably flattered to receive a letter of thanks and a polite invitation to visit the School. He complied with the invitation and a contemporary plate illustrates the subsequent proceedings in three stages. First we see him vigorously tossed in a blanket by the scholars, next he is stretched along a table, untrussed, and receiving a schoolboy birching, finally he kneels, and begs pardon in Dean's Yard.

The following year Curll attracted the attention of the future author of *Robinson Crusoe*. In an anonymous article in the *Weekly Journal* Defoe denounced Curll and all his works with a wealth of moral indignation which forestalls the efforts of certain modern journalists in a similar vein. He coined the word "Curlicism" to denote the iniquities he trounced and wanted to know why Curll's "abominable Catalogue" was not suppressed "in a Country where Religion is talk'd of (little more, God knows)." But the authorities were less easily drawn than they have been in some modern instances. It was not in Curll's nature to suffer in silence. Willingly adopting his opponent's neologism he replied with a pamphlet *Curlicism Displayed* which

Edmund Curll

under cover of defending his activities was really an impudent advertisement of his less reputable publications. His printing of Lord Essex's divorce case in a volume of his "best-seller" series, *Cases of Impotency and Divorce*, is complained of! But who drew up the original report? No less a person than Dr. George Abbot, then Archbishop of Canterbury, and presumably he did it in the public interest. What more desirable then, than that the public should have the opportunity of perusing the spicier passages as printed in detail by Curll? Again, take the objection to a translation of Meibomius's *De usu Flagrorum in re Medica et Venerea* by the late Dr. George Sewell of Hampstead (one of Curll's hacks): how could a layman, like Defoe, judge a purely medical treatise? One can hear eunuchs' singing at the Opera: what, then, is reprehensible about a book dealing with them? And so on. . . .

Defoe was silenced, and Curlicism flourished. Curll soon took service as a political spy under Sir Robert Walpole. The job was perhaps lucrative and certainly congenial; and Curll no doubt had an eye to possible protection from the bluff, hearty and broad-minded Whig Minister. This hope did not stand him in any great stead, however, in the major disaster which overtook him in 1725.

The previous autumn Curll had published a singularly scandalous book. It was a translation of a French pseudonymous publication of the previous century by

Above All Liberties

the Abbé Barrin called *Vénus dans le Cloître, ou la religieuse en chemise*. Somebody made a serious complaint to the authorities and Curll got wind of coming trouble. He hastily printed *The Humble Representation of Edmund Curll, Bookseller and Stationer of London, Concerning Five Books, complained of to the Secretary of State*. A good move, no doubt! But the trouble was that the *Representation* was not really humble at all, but a defence and exposition of his works hardly less saucy than his reply to Defoe. The blow fell in March. Curll was arrested on account of two of the books objected to: *Venus in the Cloister or the Nun in her Smock* and the Meibomius previously referred to. Curll did not obtain bail till July, and in November he stood his trial before the King's Bench at Westminster Hall. It appears that everybody (except Curll) speedily agreed that he was *homo iniquus et sceleratus*. But was that a punishable offence? His counsel moved in arrest of judgment on the ground that it was not a libel and, if punishable at all, was a matter for the Spiritual Courts. The Lord Chief Justice seemed clear that a matter in writing could not be the concern of the Spiritual Courts. There was considerable argument among the judges. Curll in his lowly position may have followed enough of it to hope that he would fall neatly between two stools. Read's case gave the Bench a lot of trouble. The Attorney-General insisted that to corrupt the morals of the King's subjects was an offence at Common Law. The King's

Edmund Curll

peace could be broken without *vi et armes*. If you destroyed morality, he argued, you destroyed the peace of Government. At last the Lord Chief Justice decided that the case was of such great consequence that it must stand over for fuller argument. Curll left the Court on bail—a guilty but unsentenced man.

He went off in a huff. If he could not publish what books he chose, he would publish none. Prudence also counselled a graceful retreat. Accordingly a solemn apology and announcement of his retirement appeared in the newspapers. He would never offend again. The Old Adam was, however, hard of dying. It was only reasonable that he should finish off two books "now in the Press" before he went, and he could not resist the temptation to announce them in his valedictory statement. One of the two happened to be *The Case of Seduction translated from the French by Mr. Rogers being the late Proceedings at Paris against the Rev. Abbé des Rues*. . . .

Soon after this ill-advised announcement Curll was re-arrested, his shop raided and nine books and pamphlets seized. In his prison Curll turned reformer and wrote a pamphlet called *The Prisoner's Advocate*, exposing abuses with which his position made him only too well acquainted.

It was July 1726 before (apparently thanks to Walpole) he was on bail again. Counsel managed to get his case postponed till the following year, but even prison could not keep him out of mischief. Before his

Above All Liberties

release he had become involved in publishing some political memoirs of a "seditious and scandalous" character. Jacobite tendencies were even more serious in the eyes of his judges than bawdry.

In Curll's favour it was argued that *The Nun in her Smock* had been published as long ago as 1683 by Henry Rhodes, a noted Bookseller in Fleet Street. But Rhodes had had no powerful enemies, or political black marks. All Curll's twists and turns could not save him from coming up for judgment on February 13, 1739. We hear no more of the legal argument or his initial offences. He is fined twice: once for the moral offences and once for the political offence, and ordered to stand in the pillory for one hour in addition *for the latter*. It is interesting to note the precise terms of the sentence, for it has been repeatedly stated (and by good authorities) that Curll stood in the pillory for publishing obscene books, but this is not true. He wore "the wooden ruff" as it was called for a political misdemeanour.

The pillory was no joke. Even an hour of it could be an unpleasant experience. By law the populace could throw anything but stones, and when so minded, they made the most of their opportunities for displaying their disapproval of the culprit. Not long before Curll's turn some unfortunates whose offences upset the professional susceptibilities of the Ladies of Drury Lane were lucky to escape from the pillory with their lives. It was only the previous May that an elderly

Edmund Curll

man had stood in the pillory right in front of Curll's shop. In spite of all the efforts of the victim's friends, and in spite of the fact that he "had got Armour under his Cloathes, and an Iron Cap under his Hat," he had to be taken down after half an hour to prevent his being murdered. And Curll's windows had been broken! Naturally he took his own precautions for his forthcoming appearance. A broadsheet was prepared for the mob who were flatteringly addressed as "Gentlemen." Their reverence for the late Queen Anne was played on, and it was cunningly suggested that the "Gentleman who now appears before you" had been guilty of nothing except excessive zeal for the good memory of the departed Monarch. Thrust into the hands of the crowd who assembled at Charing Cross on February 23, 1728, this ingenious document had the desired effect. One man exercised his constitutional privilege and threw an egg. He was nearly lynched. The wily Curll left the pillory unscathed.

After these troubles he found himself in low water for a time, but Pope's attack in the *Dunciad* came as a whiff of oxygen to his flagging fortune. He counter-attacked with spirit and became a sort of leader of those "dunces" who were not prepared to take their chastisement lying down. This pamphleteering helped to reline Curll's pockets. The long, long quarrel with Pope no sooner died down than it took on fresh life—and Curll always exploited it to his profit. Then, of course, copies of *The Case of Seduction* could always

Above All Liberties

be trotted out when a clergyman got into hot water. In one of his better moods we find him collaborating with some learned Fellows of Oxford University over the issue of a series of volumes on English antiquities.

Our subject does not require us to follow this incorrigible, but game, rogue to his grave in 1747. Our interest in Curll is chiefly concerned with the fact that in 1727, nineteen years after Read's case, his prosecution authoritatively established the publication of obscenity as an offence at Common Law. No Act of Parliament had been passed. The law was judge-made law. The change in that nineteen years is a good illustration of that chameleon-like property of English law of which we shall see more later on and which has been exemplified in more than one branch in recent times.

The case illustrates two aspects of the moral censorship of literature which are worthy of note. One is the connection between that censorship and politics, a connection which has been much more important in France than here. The other is the fact that "obscenity" or "pornography" are by no means clear-cut terms indicating something of indubitable moral worthlessness. In English law courts it is customary to speak of a vendor of pornography as necessarily a man of low type (for some reason he is generally "foreign") and his wares as totally repulsive. But Curll's case already shows that things are not so simple as that. Curll was undoubtedly a rascal: but there were sides

Edmund Curll

to his character which won him the respectful attention of earnest and scholarly men. He undoubtedly selected many of his wares for no other reason than for their appeal to salacious tastes. But the two books for which he was convicted were by no means ephemeral trash. Meibomius's treatise has its place in the history of medicine; and *The Nun* started her career as a Protestant tract on the religious controversies of France. Thus we see, even at this early stage, that the web the law was weaving promised many a tangle and many a contradiction.

CHAPTER III

THE MAKING OF A LAW

DURING the eighteenth century the law of obscene libel as established by Curll's case was a sort of poor relation in the libel family. Little is heard of it, and when it does appear it is generally in the role of a hanger-on to its more substantial cousins, seditious libel and blasphemous libel. At the end of the century, however, an astonishing change came over English literature. From being as outspoken as any other, in about twenty years it became so strait-laced as to be an historical curiosity. The change is well illustrated by an anecdote related by Sir Walter Scott in one of his letters:[1]

A grand-aunt of my own, Mrs. Keith of Ravelstone, who was a person of some condition, being a daughter of Sir John Swinton—lived with unabated vigour of intellect to a very advanced age. She was very fond of reading, and enjoyed it to the last of her long life. One day she asked me, when we happened to be alone together, whether I had ever seen Mrs. Behn's novels?—I confessed the charge.—Whether I could get her a sight of them?—I said, with some hesitation, I believed I could; but that I did not think she would like either the manners, or the language, which approached too near that of Charles II's time to be quite proper reading. "Nevertheless," said the good old lady, "I remember them being so much

[1] Lockhart's *Life*, 1839 ed., vol. vi, p. 406.

The Making of a Law

admired, and being so much interested in them myself, that I wish to look at them again." To hear was to obey. So I sent Mrs. Aphra Behn, curiously sealed up, with "private and confidential" on the packet, to my gay old grandaunt. The next time I saw her afterwards, she gave me back Aphra, properly wrapped up, with nearly these words: "Take back your bonny Mrs. Behn; and, if you will take my advice, put her in the fire, for I found it impossible to get through the very first novel. But is it not," she said, "a very odd thing that I, an old woman of eighty and upwards, sitting alone, feel myself ashamed to read a book which, sixty years ago, I have heard read aloud for the amusement of large circles, consisting of the finest and most creditable society in London."

In his Preface (1850) to *The History of Pendennis* Thackeray writes:

Since the author of *Tom Jones* was buried, no writer of fiction among us has been permitted to depict to his utmost power a MAN. We must drape him, and give him a certain conventional simper. Society will not tolerate the Natural in our Art. Many ladies have remonstrated and subscribers left me, because, in the course of the story, I described a young man resisting and affected by temptation. My object was to say, that he had the passions to feel, and the manliness and generosity to overcome them. You will not hear—it is best to know it—what moves in the real world, what passes in society, in the clubs, colleges, news'-rooms—what is the life and talk of your sons. A little more frankness than is customary has been attempted in this story; with no bad desire on the writer's part, it is hoped, and with no ill consequence to any reader.

Above All Liberties

The *Athenaeum*, a literary weekly with a scholarly and European outlook, never quoted anything from foreign literature which a young girl might not read. How the blindness to one side of human life of which Thackeray complains can distort the vision of a literary critic of eminence is illustrated by the following remarks about Dean Swift made by Augustine Birrell in his *Essays about Men, Women and Books* (1894):

No fouler pen than Swift's has soiled our literature. His language is horrible from first to last. He is full of odious images, of base and abominable allusions. It would be a labour of Hercules to cleanse his pages. His love-letters are defaced by his incurable coarseness. This habit of his is so inveterate that it seems a miracle he kept his sermons free from blackguard phrases. It is a question not of morality, but of decency, whether it is becoming to sit in the same room with the works of this divine. How the good Sir Walter ever managed to see him through the press is amazing. In this matter Swift is inexcusable.

Birrell subsequently became President of the Board of Education. His finicky and asexual attitude to life and letters is typical of the Liberal movement in which he played his part.

The change we are considering was not in any way effected by law. It was a change in public opinion. The law of obscene libel did not at the time concern itself with anything that by any stretch of imagination could be called literature. It fought a not very successful battle with a flood of gross pornography which

The Making of a Law

appears to have increased as reputable literature grew more prudish. But this battle attracted more and more attention both public and judicial. The day of the "purity" society had arrived. The existence of obscene libel began to be recognised in various Acts of Parliament dealing with local government and vagrancy. At last, in 1857 Lord Chief Justice Campbell secured the passing of the Obscene Publications Act. It cannot be too firmly insisted that this Act is *not* the basis of the law concerning literary obscenity. The Act created no new offence. It was a preventive Act which sought to forestall the sale of obscene books by providing for their destruction by justices of the peace. The Lord Chief Justice was emphatic that it did not alter the common law and would not be used against anything but gross pornography.

Nine years after, however, the common law was changed, not by Act of Parliament but by a judge, or perhaps it would be truer to say, by the authors of legal text-books. There had been in existence since the early years of the century a Protestant pamphlet which sought to discredit the Roman Catholic Church by quoting standard works on moral theology used by confessors. These works enter into the most intimate details of married life with a profundity of erudition and a wealth of logic that is far from edifying to the untheological mind. It is fortunate, therefore, that they are obtainable only in Latin. The pamphlet in question gave extracts from the original with English translations in parallel columns. In the course of its career it had appeared under various titles, and had even undergone some bowdlerisation out of deference, no doubt, to the temper of the time. A certain Henry Scott, a metal broker of Wolverhampton, obtained from time to time supplies of the pamphlet (at the time entitled *The Confessional Unmasked*) from "The Protestant Electoral Union." Out of religious zeal he sold them to all comers at the price he paid for them—one shilling each. In 1867 the justices of Wolverhampton made an order that his stock of two hundred and fifty copies which had been seized under Lord Campbell's Act should be destroyed. Scott appealed to Quarter Sessions and the Recorder, a Benjamin Hicklin, found in his favour on the ground that although the pamphlet was obscene and its indiscriminate sale and circulation was calculated to prejudice good morals, his motive in selling it was the innocent one of promoting the objects of the Protestant Electoral Union and exposing the error of the Church of Rome, particularly as regards the confessional. The Catholics did not, of course, take this lying down, and there was an appeal to the Queen's Bench *sub nomen R.* v. *Hicklin*. The question for decision was: If it be granted that a book is obscene and its publication likely to prejudice good morals, is such publication lawful because the publisher's object was a lawful one? The answer of the Court was "No." But it is not that decision which makes

The Making of a Law

the case important. In the course of his judgment Lord Chief Justice Cockburn gave his opinion as to what "obscenity" was. His words were clearly *obiter dicta*, and therefore not binding as law, since the issue of obscenity was not before the Court, the Recorder having admitted the obscenity of the pamphlet. Nevertheless the Cockburn definition was repeated in the text-books and accepted as established law. Here it is:

> The test of obscenity is this, whether the tendency of the matter charged as obscenity is to deprave and corrupt those whose minds are open to such immoral influences and into whose hands a publication of this sort may fall.

Clearly, if consistently applied, this definition would reduce literature to the level of the nursery. Arbitrarily applied it has proved a fruitful source of injustice to individuals and of damage to science, literature and society.

The increasing scope of the "obscenity" law during the nineteenth century was part of a more general process whereby the Industrial Revolution spread a harsh, mechanised, and joyless puritanism wherever its influence was felt. Even in the remote Highlands of Scotland native art, music, dancing and a certain dignified gaiety were ruthlessly stamped out by Presbyterian "missionaries" from the Lowlands. In the Introduction to his *Carmina Gadelica*, Alexander Carmichael records a distressing incident related to

Above All Liberties

him during one of his visits to the Hebrides which is more revealing than a host of generalities. A young lady told him:

> When we came to Islay I was sent to the parish school to obtain a proper grounding in arithmetic. I was charmed with the schoolgirls and their Gaelic songs. But the schoolmaster—an alien like myself—denounced Gaelic speech and Gaelic songs. On getting out of school one evening the girls resumed a song they had been singing the previous evening. I joined willingly, if timidly, my knowledge of Gaelic being small. The schoolmaster heard us, however, and called us back. He punished us till the blood trickled from our fingers, although we were big girls, with the dawn of womanhood upon us. The thought of that scene thrills me with indignation.

We may note that the indignation of English evacuees over the use of the tawse in Scottish schools initiated an illuminating correspondence in the *Scotsman* during January and February 1941.

The new interpretation of the law was invoked against Charles Bradlaugh and Annie Besant for republishing a pamphlet on contraception which had been in circulation for forty years. Bradlaugh's skill as a lawyer won the day, but the case left no less a jurist than Sir James Stephen apprehensive lest an *ex post facto* censorship of the press had not been set up so far as even serious publications on the relations of the sexes were concerned.

But if the wily Bradlaugh escaped, Sir James

The Making of a Law

Stephen's apprehension was more than justified by the case of Havelock Ellis. A study of his life and work will exemplify better than anything the grave implications of a body of law developed from nothing by judges, law book writers and an uncritical legislature in the space of about two centuries.

CHAPTER IV

HAVELOCK ELLIS

I

WHAT luck for a little boy of seven to go round the world in his father's ship, and that a sailing ship, too! Such was Havelock Ellis's good fortune in 1866. His father was a sea captain, and his home a happy one. This felicity was perhaps assisted by the nature of his father's occupation. A sailor's spasmodic returns to the domestic circle are often more eagerly welcome than the regular appearances of husbands who follow more sedentary callings. His mother was an Evangelical Christian of a severe school. Her convictions forbade the theatre and alcohol was not served at her board. This latter abstention did not, however, prevent Captain Ellis from drinking his little son's health with his officers in champagne when the news of the birth reached his ship at Singapore. Havelock was an only son, but he had four sisters.

On his return home he was sent to a small school, where among other things he learnt dancing. In later life he attributed to the dance an important place in the scheme of life. His pacific nature was demonstrated in a very early incident. One day he came home with a noticeable hole in the back of his neck. By questioning him, his mother learnt that it had been made with a sharp slate-pencil by one of his companions. Indignantly she said, "I hope you paid him back." "No," replied Havelock, "for then I should have been as bad as he was."

Next he attended the "French and German College" at Merton, where he remained until he was twelve. Here he acquired an early acquaintance with modern languages which was later to prove a great boon to him. Although European thought can still be regarded as a unity, it is a unity which diversity of language makes it extremely difficult for one man to master. This has been particularly so in recent times when translation has declined both in quality and quantity. In the field of study that Ellis was to choose for his own, this is specially so. Only a small proportion of first-rate sexological works are translated into English; and the translations that are made are frequently poor and unscholarly.

From twelve to sixteen he was a weekly boarder at an exclusive school at Mitcham. He showed early signs of promise and became an indefatigable notetaker. It is worthy of remark that sport had no interest for him. According to Houston Peterson's biography: "At best he was a serious youth, apparently destined for an honourable career in a conservative church. At worst he was a sententious, unworldly little prig too much concerned with God and duty."

At sixteen his sex curiosity was awakened. Such

Above All Liberties

curiosity was by no means easy to satisfy at the time. Even the great Huxley's *Elementary Physiology* dared make no mention of the processes of human reproduction. At this age Havelock was ignorant of girls, he had experienced nothing of the corruption frequently associated with boarding-schools, and his reading had been entirely conventional.

Anxiety about his health caused him to be placed once more on board his father's ship, this time for a rest-cure. During the long voyage to Australia he read extensively. Under the influence of Shelley his orthodox faith began to crumble and was soon gone.

He plunged into Swinburne, but it is characteristic that the poet's revolutionary enthusiasm moved him little. In after-life Ellis was never bitterly hostile to any religious expression nor bound up in any political issue. As a result of reading Rabelais, he took a long farewell of prudery and became free of that famous Abbey of Thelème, "in whose rule," he tells us in *Affirmations*, "was but one clause, *Fait ce que vouldras*, a rule which no pagan or Christian had ever set up before, because never before, except as involved in the abstract conceptions of philosophers, had the thought of voluntary co-operation of the unsolicited freedom to do well appeared before European men."

In the South Atlantic an incident occurred which illustrates the quiet courage which always distinguished Ellis. An exceptionally heavy wave broke

Havelock Ellis

over the stern destroying instruments and furniture and flooding the cabin occupied by Havelock and his father. Had they been in it at the time they would probably both have been killed. The son's only comment was: "Does this often happen, father?"

When the ship reached Sydney it was decided that, in the state of Havelock's health, it was undesirable that he should continue the voyage on to Calcutta. So it was arranged that he should remain and await his father's return. As things turned out, he stayed four years.

For a great deal of this time he earned his livelihood by teaching, and much of it was spent in small settlements where he was almost alone. Erotic physical manifestations began to obtrude themselves on his notice, particularly, he tells us, in association with a reading of Brantôme's *Vie des Dames Galantes*. He was more and more tormented by the problems of sex, and one evening, in 1875, under the eucalyptus trees in the school grounds of Burwood, he made the most important resolution of his life. He would devote himself to a study of the matters that perplexed him in order that future generations of young people should be spared his sufferings. In the Preface to the first published volume of his celebrated *Studies* he wrote:

> The origin of these studies dates from many years back. As a youth I was faced, as others are, by the problem of sex. Living partly in an Australian city where the ways of life were plainly seen, partly in the solitude of the bush, I

Above All Liberties

was free both to contemplate and to meditate many things. A resolve slowly grew up within me: one part of my life-work should be to make clear the problems of sex. That was more than twenty years ago. Since then I can honestly say that in all that I have done that resolve has never been very far from my thoughts.

His self-appointed task could not be said to be completed until fifty years after, when he finished the seventh and supplementary volume of the *Studies*.

Ellis's early steps on this long road were facilitated by a fortunate chance. He came across a copy of George Drysdale's *Elements of Social Science* in the window of a Sydney book-shop. This work was first published in 1854 under the title *Physical, Sexual and Natural Religion*, and had been issued in a third and enlarged edition in the year of Ellis's birth. The book never attracted a great deal of popular attention, and during the lifetime of its author it did not bear his name. Nevertheless, it went quietly from edition to edition, and was translated into every European language. It was an early attempt to face the problems of sex in an honest, scientific and rational spirit. In spite of some inaccuracies due to its early date, it is a most valuable treatise, and Ellis was indeed lucky to possess it.

But Ellis was by no means entirely occupied with his chosen subjects. His reading included the great novelists of European literature, and *Wilhelm Meister*

Havelock Ellis

was his great consolation. He matriculated at Sydney University; and by study and literary exercise laid the foundations of his career as an author. He started the commonplace books which he industriously compiled for ten years, and began writing poetry which he continued until 1885.

The extent to which poets have dedicated their lives to the muses has greatly varied. There are those who are poets before all else, who have steeped themselves in the poetic tradition, and whose highest ambition has been to weave from an essentially literary experience further additions to, and developments of, that tradition. Of such Swinburne, Pound and Eliot are outstanding examples. At the other end of the scale are men, commoner in less specialised ages than our own, who have been pre-eminently something other than poets, but whose experiences have been so vital that their expression has been forced to assume poetic form. Havelock Ellis is of that order.

His life-work was the great *Studies in the Psychology of Sex*, but the breadth of the man's mind and achievement is not fully appreciated. He is in many quarters regarded as a worker in a narrow field, and his books looked upon as meet for the specialist alone. The truth is that just as he approached the problem of sex by way of its exceptional manifestations, so he made the study of sex the key to an understanding of life itself. He stands to be judged as a great philosopher.

Many of his sonnets (together with some charming

Above All Liberties

translations of Spanish folk-songs) were published in 1925 and some of the sonnets[1] reprinted in 1937. They express the depth and breadth of an apprehension of beauty and form which fired a young man "to maintain the causes of freedom and order" (his own words) in a field where chaos and superstition reigned supreme. Wearied by the spiritual aridity of Shaw, and the futilities of Wells, modern youth has shown a tendency to turn to the worn-out nostrums of the bishops or the modern quackery of the Buchmanites. It may be that before it is too late they will learn from Ellis that the fullest development of beauty and nobility in human life is quite consistent with scientific truth and intellectual integrity.

During Ellis's exile he was much influenced by the work of James Hinton, a medical man and philosopher in the line of William Blake who had died the year that Ellis set foot on Australian soil. Ellis saw that he, too, must study medicine, and so great was the effect of Hinton's philosophy on his mind that he described it as a "conversion." This is not the place to examine this remarkable psychological phenomenon. We can only compare it with the effect of Spinoza on Goethe, of Wordsworth on J. S. Mill, and of Schopenhauer on Nietzsche; and say that so profound were its repercussions that in no fundamental sense did Ellis develop after 1878. His view of the nature of the universe

---

[1] "Madonna" throws light on the author's particular sensibility. Compare *My Life*, pp. 67–70.

Havelock Ellis

and of his own place in it was settled when he was nineteen.

This period of exile, solitude and germination came to an end in 1879 when he returned home. A short novel entitled *Kanga Creek* written after his return and published in 1922 describes in poetic fashion his life in Australia.

Returning to his home at the age of twenty he was not unnaturally something of a hero to his mother and four sisters. The subsequent decade up to the publication of his first book in 1890 was a period of intense activity in which it seemed that energy stored up during the previous four years came to flower and fruit.

He managed to secure the means to finance a medical training and worked hard, walking St. Thomas's Hospital for nine years. Here he obtained first-hand knowledge of the evils of poverty, and saw bitter evidence of the need for the spread of birth-control among the masses of the people.

The eighties were a time of great social ferment and Ellis moved among the advanced, socialist and progressive society of the day. He assisted in the formation of two progressive associations. One of these made a collection of secular hymns for use at their meetings. Ellis made a contribution beginning:

> Onward, brothers, march still onward,
> March still onward hand in hand;
> Till ye see at last Man's Kingdom,
> Till ye reach the Promised Land.

Above All Liberties

Ellis sometimes playfully suggested that this inanity would survive all his other works. The other association, "The Fellowship of the New Life," attempted an experiment in communal living; and some of its more politically-minded members, including Bernard Shaw, left to found the Fabian Society. It is worthy of note that in spite of activity of this type, Ellis hardly ever gave a lecture or an address in his life.

While Ellis was living in the Australian bush, far away on the Great Karroo of South Africa another genius was maturing. Olive Schreiner, the daughter of a German missionary, grew up in a wild and pioneer environment. She used her leisure and alleviated her solitude by writing novels. By saving her earnings as a governess she was able to come to England in 1881. One of the novels, *The Story of an African Farm*, was published three years later. The book found a responsive reader in Ellis; he wrote to the authoress and soon after they met. The meeting resulted in a relationship which illumined this period of Ellis's life, and continued by correspondence after she returned to South Africa in 1889. It was an intimate association of intense affection which embraced intellectual as well as emotional interests. They worked together and inspired each other; but both agreed that marriage would have been inimical to their careers. After her return, Olive's genius seemed to fade. In 1894 she married an athletic sheep farmer who was Ellis's opposite in every way. In 1917 she

Havelock Ellis

distressed Ellis by demanding the return of her letters to him. Ellis set a high literary value on these letters, but in the end he agreed to burn the later ones.

At the beginning of this period Ellis discovered Walt Whitman. He met Edward Carpenter through reading *Towards Democracy* and formed a warm friendship which lasted until Carpenter's death in 1929.

In 1886 Ellis obtained from Henry Vizetelly a commission as general editor of a series of unexpurgated texts of the old English dramatists. The first volume of the Mermaid Series, as it was called, appeared the following year. It consisted of Marlowe's plays and a general introduction by John Addington Symonds. An appendix contained a British Museum manuscript consisting of an information laid against Marlowe by an informer to the Privy Council. Marlowe is charged with a series of highly scandalous, blasphemous and immoral saying and views, and the document is generally known as "Marlowe's damnable opinions." It had previously been ignored by writers on Marlowe, and Ellis printed it for the first time. Ellis added a sensible note in which he put forward the suggestion that the information was a crude and ignorant version of acute and audacious utterances actually made by Marlowe and now "substantially held, more or less widely, by students of science and of the Bible in our own days." The "damnable opinions" were the cause of Ellis experiencing a pre-

Above All Liberties

liminary brush with the censorial mind. Many people were shocked, and even Swinburne and J. A. Symonds wrote expressing their disapproval. A well-meaning woman protested vigorously against the publication. Vizetelly (without consulting Ellis) replaced several words and phrases by asterisks in subsequent issues of the book, and the booksellers were provided with sets of the new leaves so that they could correct their stock.

The second volume of the series was the plays of Massinger, and Ellis secured the services of Arthur Symons as editor. Symons was a self-educated man of considerable brilliance, and Ellis formed a close friendship with him. A rather typical *fin de siècle* decadent and aesthete he provided a valuable counterpoise to Ellis's excessively idealistic and impractical nature. They travelled together a great deal: to Spain (for which country Ellis conceived a great love), to Russia and, of course, to Paris where Ellis met Verlaine, Rodin, Huysmans, Rémy de Gourmont and other choice spirits.

When the Mermaid Series had run into ten or fifteen volumes, Vizetelly was ruined by a prosecution under the obscenity law in 1888 for publishing translations of Zola. Fisher Unwin took over the series, mangled the texts, removed Ellis's name and dispensed with his further services without explanation or apology. He was more fortunate as editor of the Contemporary Science Series. This series con-

Havelock Ellis

tinued until the war of 1914 put an end to it. Many of the volumes were of the highest merit, and a considerable proportion of Ellis's modest income came from this source.

Ellis had resolved not to write a book of his own until he was thirty. According to plan, in 1890 his first book, *The New Spirit*, appeared. The new spirit was the change that had come into the world with the French Revolution, and the book consisted of studies of Diderot, Heine, Whitman, Ibsen and Tolstoy. The *Spectator* gave him a foretaste of the sort of treatment he might expect from orthodox critics. The notice began: "Mr. Havelock Ellis—if 'Mr.' be the proper title, of which we have considerable doubt," and ended, "We cannot imagine anything of which it would be more necessary for human nature to purge itself than the 'New Spirit' of Havelock Ellis."

The same year his *The Criminal*, a study written at white heat in reaction from some of Lombroso's doctrines, appeared.

The next year he married Edith Lees with whom he had been associated in his work for the "Fellowship of the New Life" and who had acquired a modest literary reputation. Of the exaltations and the corresponding frustrations of that marriage Ellis has told much in his autobiography. He speaks of his wife in these words:

What I experienced with this woman—I feel now many years after her death—was *life*. She was the instrument that brought out all those tones which the older I grow I feel to be of the very essence of life, tones of joy sometimes but oftener of anguish, not happiness. I smile when I find people cheerfully talking of "happiness" as something to be desired in life. I do not know what happiness may be, but it is not life. I have lived. And this woman by her peculiar temperament, by her acute sensibility, by her energy of impulse, by her deep hold of my most sensitive fibres, struck out the notes of joy and anguish which are love and which also are life. For love as I have known it is a passion more of what we call the soul than of the body; unlike the passion that is alone of the flesh, it is a flame that continues to burn even long years after the body that may seem to have inspired it is turned to dust. But it is because I have known love that I have lived and that my life and my work in the world have been one. My work, I am often told, is cool and serene, entirely reasonable and free of passion, but without that devouring passion of the soul my work would have been nothing.

I speak of a flame. Yet when I inhale the scent of a flower this woman loved, or gaze on a picture or a book that meant much to her, I am wrapped away from the world and caught up into another sky. I realise what are the only things in life that have any value for us and I know—what all our science as well as our art has so often asserted—that the so-called "realities" are nothing, that it is the things that are made of space and time, out of emptiness, our symbols and our pictures, that are alone the eternal things.

The marriage made no difference to his friendship with Arthur Symons. The Ellises had agreed not to live continuously under the same roof, and Havelock

Havelock Ellis

spent a good deal of his time sharing rooms with Symons in the Temple, at Fountain Court. Symons was editing *The Savoy*, the rival of *The Yellow Book*, and Ellis contributed an article on Zola. This, together with studies of Nietzsche, Casanova, Huysmans and St. Francis of Assisi, was published under the title *Affirmations* in 1897.

All this time Ellis had been collecting material for his great work. In 1894 he published a preparatory volume entitled *Man and Woman*. The manner in which he started off the *Studies* was to a large extent fortuitous. John Addington Symonds had always been interested in the subject of sexual inversion. Although the prudery of the time forbade him doing justice to this theme in the works on classical and Renaissance literature which made his name famous, he had privately published two essays on the subject. As a result of his association with Ellis over the Marlowe volume, he proposed that they should collaborate in a full-size work. Ellis was naturally flattered, and decided to make the book Volume I of his *Studies in the Psychology of Sex*.

From the beginning the book, entitled *Sexual Inversion*, was ill-fated. A few months after Symonds had made his contribution to the joint work he died. The Wilde case made rational discussion of homosexuality in this country even more difficult than ever. Failing an English publisher, the book appeared in German from Leipzig in 1896. The great value of the

Above All Liberties

book lay not so much in any original suggestion or discovery as in the example it gave of patient and scientific treatment. The detailed case-histories it contained were an important addition to knowledge. They were the first British cases unconnected with asylums or prisons ever recorded.

Ellis at last found an English publisher in the engaging but shady person of the pseudonymous "Dr. Villiers." No sooner had the English version come from the press than Symonds' executors forbade the use of his name and material. So the edition had to be withdrawn and another with only Ellis's name and contribution printed. The circumstances in which this book fell foul of the law of obscene libel are fully explained in my *The Banned Books of England*. George Bedborough, the Secretary of a reformist body called The Legitimation League, with which Ellis had no connection, was indicted at the Old Bailey for selling the book. He was persuaded by the police, who made promises of lenient treatment, to plead "Guilty." The book was thus suppressed and the author by implication condemned as a common pornographer without being able to say a word in his own defence.

At the trial the Recorder of London, Sir Charles Hall, sat as judge. He addressed Bedborough in these words: "You might at the outset perhaps have been gulled into the belief that somebody might say that this was a scientific book. But it is impossible for anybody with a head on his shoulders to open the book without seeing that it is a pretence and a sham, and that it is merely entered into for the purpose of selling this filthy publication." The next day the *Daily Chronicle*, of which Henry Massingham was editor, came out with a leader that while giving Ellis credit for "scientific intentions" substantially supported the Recorder. Ellis in *My Life* comments as follows:

Law and the Press were indeed well matched, and between them they thought that they had dismissed me and my book from the world. Yet I—rather the spirit of Man I chanced to embody—have overcome the world. My "filthy" and "worthless" and "morbid" book has been translated into all the greatest living languages to reach people who could not say what a Recorder is, nor read the *Daily Chronicle* even if they saw it. Unto this day it continues to bring me from many lands the reverent and grateful words of strangers whose praise keeps me humble in the face of the supreme mystery of life.

Ellis's immediate reaction to this affront was stated in a little pamphlet entitled *A Note on the Bedborough Trial* written soon afterwards. It contains the following passage:

Under these circumstances, therefore, the difficulties of publishing the remaining volumes of my *Studies in the Psychology of Sex* in England are sufficiently obvious, and the decision I have been forced to reach seems inevitable. To wrestle in the public arena for freedom of speech is a noble task which may worthily be undertaken by any man who can devote to it the best energies of his life. It is not, however, a task which I have ever contemplated. I am a student, and my path has been long marked out. I may be forced to pursue it under unfavourable conditions, but I do not intend that any consideration shall induce me to swerve from it, nor do I intend to injure my work or distort my vision of life by entering upon any struggle. The pursuit of the martyr's crown is not favourable to the critical and dispassionate investigation of complicated problems. A student of nature, of men, of books, may dispense with wealth or position; he cannot dispense with quietness and serenity. I insist on doing my own work in my own way, and cannot accept conditions which make this work virtually impossible. Certainly I regret that my own country should be almost alone in refusing to me the conditions of reasonable intellectual freedom. I regret it the more since I deal with the facts of English life, and prefer to address English people. But I must leave to others the task of obtaining the reasonable freedom that I am unable to attain.

And so the work went on. Copies of the second volume found their way into an English law court and were duly condemned along with a translation of Charles Féré's *La Pathologie des Émotions*. But volume after volume appeared in the States, and copies percolated all over the world, even into this country. At last the sixth volume was published in 1910. In his pocket diary for August 7th of the previous year, Ellis recorded the completion of the manuscript by a quotation from the great Elizabethan, George Chapman: "The work that I was born to do is done."

We may note that he was only able to carry on in this way by taking advantage of the legal diversities

Havelock Ellis

caused by nationalist divisions. The evils caused by these divisions have been greatly stressed of recent times. But we must not lose sight of the fact that freedom sometimes flourishes through diversity and lack of logic. One of the minor aims of the League of Nations (in which it was often more successful than in the pursuit of its major aims) was the uniform enforcement of obscenity laws all over the world. The success of this aim would have rendered the remedy that was open to Ellis in his trouble no longer effective.

Ellis regarded the sixth volume of the Studies as completing his task. The twenty years between his first book and this sixth volume may be said to be the summer of his life. At fifty Ellis experienced a curious impression of premature old age. This impression was enhanced by the failure of his wife's health in 1915 and her death in the following year. In fact, in 1909 Ellis had thirty years of life before him; but these years must be regarded as his autumn. But they were a prolific autumn. Besides a seventh and supplementary volume to the *Studies*, published in 1926, he produced a mass of other work. He wrote *Little Essays of Love and Virtue* in 1922 for the youths and girls whose welfare was always before his mind when engaged on the more difficult *Studies*. In 1928 he summarised his philosophy in *The Dance of Life*, and in 1934 he published an introductory text-book entitled *The Psychology of Sex*.

Above All Liberties

During the autumn of his life he was rewarded by acknowledgment of his merits and international fame. The Royal College of Physicians, to their credit, made a tardy tribute to his lifelong devotion to scholarship by making him a Fellow. But no English university, it is worthy of note, honoured itself by honouring him. The appraisement of a foreigner is often more significant than that of a fellow countryman. This is what H. L. Mencken, the distinguished American critic, said[1] about Ellis:

If the test of the personal culture of a man be the degree of freedom from banal ideas and childish emotions which move the great masses of men, then Havelock Ellis is undoubtedly the most civilised Englishman of his generation.

He is a man of the soundest and widest learning, but it is not his positive learning that gives him distinction; it is his profound and implacable skepticism, his penetrating eye for the transient, the disingenuous and the shoddy. So unconditioned a skepticism, it must be plain, is not an English habit. The average Englishman of science, though he may challenge the Continentals within his speciality, is only too apt to sink to the level of a politician, a greengrocer, or a suburban clergyman outside it. The examples of Wallace, Crookes and Lodge are anything but isolated. Scratch an English naturalist and you are likely to discover a spiritualist; take an English metaphysican to where the band is playing, and if he begins to snuffle patriotically you need not be surprised. The late war uncovered this weakness in a wholesale manner.

Ellis, it seems to me, stood above all the rest, and precisely because his dissent from the prevailing imbecilities

[1] Quoted from Goldberg's biography.

Havelock Ellis

was quite devoid of emotion and had nothing in it of brummagen moral purpose. . . . Ellis kept his head throughout. An Englishman of the oldest native stock, an unapologetic lover of English scenes and English ways, an unshaken believer in the essential soundness and high historical destiny of his people, he simply stood aside[1] from the current clown-show and waited in patience for sense and decency to be restored. . . . There is something almost of Renaissance dignity in his chronicle of his speculations. The man that emerges is not a mere scholar immured in a cell, but a man of the world superior to his race and time—a philosopher viewing the childish passion of lesser men disdainfully and yet not too remote to understand it, and even to see in it a certain cosmic use. . . . He is the complete anti-Kipling. In him the Huxleian tradition comes to full flavour. . . . His style . . . takes on a sort of glowing clarity. It is English that is as transparent as a crystal, and yet it is English that is full of fine colours and cadences. There could be no better investiture for the questionings and conclusions of so original, so curious, so learned, and above all, so sound and hearty a man.

In 1938 Havelock Ellis suffered a severe illness. Although he recovered he seemed to realise that the end was not far off, and he employed the small measure of his recovered health and strength in setting his affairs in order.

One task was the disposal of his extensive collection of books. I write "collection of books" rather than "library" because Havelock Ellis had little of the bibliophile about him. Although he possessed hun-

---

[1] But cf. *My Life*, p. 408.

dreds of volumes from all over the world, he appeared to care little for books as books. He kept them in no formal order, but relied on his remarkable memory to guide him to any reference he required. It was in connection with this disposal that I was privileged to see something of him during the following year, when his health made him more of a recluse than ever. He asked me to help in disposing of his rarer sexological books, and in carrying out his wishes with regard to some hundred volumes I had to visit him both at his house at Herne Hill and at his country cottage near Haywards Heath. Soon after he gave up both places and retired to Suffolk, a county in which many of his forebears had spent their lives. The hope that he would there enjoy a long and tranquil evening to his life was unhappily disappointed, and he died on Saturday, July 8, 1939.

I had met him previously in connection with my own work, and received most generous assistance including loans of books and little gifts of pamphlets. His last kindness to me was an autographed copy of his poems.

During these last years, his bodily weakness did not impair the interest of his conversation. Over lunch one sunny day at Haywards Heath he recalled his childhood, and how he once stole pennies to buy pears, his favourite fruit. On another occasion he talked about his voyages, ending up by saying: "I liked the sailing ships best." He spoke very sadly of

Havelock Ellis

Edward Carpenter's last days of infirmity, and mentioned that Mrs. Ellis used to go and stay with him, adding (characteristically): "But I would never stay away anywhere." He once complained that the French translation of his great work was a little too light in tone. I ventured to observe that it was difficult to be unduly solemn about love in the French tongue.

There was no trace of "anecdotage" in his talk. He showed a keen appreciation of present trends and controversies. Only about the Surrealists he once shook his head in a puzzled way and said: "They are beyond me." He displayed not the least bitterness with regard to the indignities to which his work had been subjected, but seemed to have a simple and complete faith in the ultimate triumph of reason and intellectual freedom.

Humbug and misrepresentation pursued Ellis to the grave. The *Times* obituary represented him as first and foremost an essayist and critic "who will also be remembered for his pioneer work in the psychology of sex." His sexological work and the trial which was such an important event in his life were only dealt with in small print in the lower part of the column. In point of fact, his essays and criticisms, elegant and stimulating as they are, were the by-products of his great work and of his courageous and unflinching demand for order and reason in a field which is still taboo to the columnists of the *Times*.

Above All Liberties

The Times Literary Supplement of October 4, 1940, devoted several columns to the centenary of J. A. Symonds' birth without mentioning Symonds' connection with Ellis over his work on inversion. Elsewhere, throughout the press of the world his greatness and his triumphs received their due mead of appreciation.

II

I have dealt with Havelock Ellis at some length in order that it may be manifest what manner of man it was that the law of obscene libel chose for its most distinguished victim; and what manner of work it was in which the English legal profession, to their eternal shame, could see nothing but pornographic abnormality.

The condemnation of 1897 kept the work out of general circulation in this country for forty years. In 1936 for the first time the *Studies in the Psychology of Sex* was openly issued in England, and its vital information and luminous wisdom is still only available for those who can afford to pay four guineas. Hardly a lending library will stock the work. What would have been the state of knowledge of natural history in this country at the end of the last century if the Bishops who considered *The Origin of Species* a work of the devil in 1859 had been able to restrict its publication to small sections of the privileged classes?

Havelock Ellis

It would be a great pity if the richly deserved tributes paid at long last to Havelock Ellis's greatness and to his triumphs conveyed the impression that the battle against prudery to which he devoted his life has been won. That is the last thing he would have wished.

The law which in effect condemned him as a common pornographer remains unrepentant. In so far as it has been changed, it has been changed for the worse. Nowadays not only offending books themselves, but their authors, publishers, and printers are usually haled before the police courts. Previously trial by jury was the rule if the persons as well as the books were attacked; now "three successful tradesmen or one unsuccessful barrister," as it has been put, are deemed enough.

Summary and harsh as the law is, it does not seem to be sufficiently so for the authorities. In 1923 the Government introduced in the House of Commons a Criminal Justice Bill dealing mainly with alterations in legal procedure. Among its many clauses was one (Clause 19) dealing with obscenity. The first paragraph of the clause read as follows:

> If a justice is satisfied by information on oath made before him by an inspector of police or any other officer of police of equal or superior rank that there is reasonable cause to suspect that indecent or obscene articles are kept within any place within the jurisdiction of the justice for the purpose of being sold, published, distributed, exhibited,

Above All Liberties

lent on hire or otherwise dealt with, and whether in any case for purposes of gain or not, the justice may issue a search warrant, authorising the constable named in the warrant to enter the place named in the warrant at any time, and, if need be, by force, and to examine the said place and any person found therin and search for any such articles therein and to seize and remove any such articles found therein.

Subsequent paragraphs provided for destruction by a Court of Summary Jurisdiction and appeal to Quarter Sessions on the same lines as the Obscene Publications Act of 1857. It is to be noted, however, that a safeguard which the House of Commons inserted into that Act was missing. The safeguard provided that no warrant could issue until a common law offence (usually a sale) had been sworn to. Furthermore the final paragraph of the Clause provided that "articles" included books, writings, pictures and models, and all other articles and things whatsoever whether similar to the things mentioned or not. It was feared by many reformers that this sweeping definition would be used to seize birth-control appliances.[1] It is a pleasure to record that this tyrannous clause was not passed into law. But the mere fact that the authorities had the temerity to insert it into the Bill throws a revealing light on their state of mind and provides a startling example of the need for the most careful scrutiny of new legislation in the interests of liberty.

[1] *New Generation*, November 1923.

Havelock Ellis

As it stands the law has proved efficient for the suppression of works of undoubted literary merit. Since Ellis's case other authors of indubitable integrity have been attacked. D. H. Lawrence's *Rainbow* was suppressed in 1915 and the manuscript of *Pansies* confiscated in 1929. In the next chapter we shall see to what extreme lengths the law can go in its control over literary expression.

Scientific works continue to be attacked. For instance, in 1921 a very interesting book from the psychoanalytical point of view, entitled *The Autobiography of a Child*, by an anonymous author was condemned. In 1935 came the conviction for "publishing an obscene libel" of the publishers of Edward Charles's *The Sexual Impulse*, in spite of the fact that sixteen expert witnesses, including scientists, religious and social workers, and literary men, went into the witness-box to testify to the scientific, educational and social value of his work. There is room for legitimate difference of opinion as to its ultimate value. But what is there to be said for a law which places any book with a sexual content at the mercy of magistrates who, however "learned" in law, appear to glory in their ignorance of science and literature? In fiction the list of reputable authors whose work has been condemned is a long and discreditable one.

Translations into English from other tongues seem to have received special attention. Before the last war, for instance, Sir Albert de Rutzen condemned a trans-

Above All Liberties

lation of Balzac's *Les Contes Drolatiques*. A translation of part of the *Greek Anthology* was condemned in 1934. In the latter case, the magistrate (provoking, no doubt, some laughter in the Elysian fields) proclaimed that "a classical author might lapse into obscenity." The law results in many classical and important foreign works being either unobtainable in complete and veracious English or obtainable only at prohibitive prices. The average reader is left with a very false impression of the Greek and Roman mind, and of the work of certain distinguished foreign authors. All the sorry farce by which the Customs authorities sought to prevent Englishmen from reading James Joyce's *Ulysses* has been repeated in the case of Henry Millar. Like *Ulysses*, his first novel, *Tropic of Cancer*, was printed in Paris. It is a vivid and vital description of the life of down-and-out American émigrés in Paris. It has been treated as a serious contribution to literature by such eminent critics as T. S. Eliot, Ezra Pound, Aldous Huxley and Montgomery Belgion. Yet both it and Millar's last book, *Tropic of Capricorn*, are banned by the Customs. It is safe to predict that the banning will have as much, and no more, effect than that of *Ulysses*.

The treatment to which Ellis's work was subjected is part of a general movement which has kept informed discussion and speculation on sexual problems out of the reach, not only of the masses, but of the general reading public. It has had deplorable results.

Havelock Ellis

During the nineteenth century the more enlightened members of all classes of society learned to think for themselves about religion, politics and economics. This spread of liberalism has had results in the amelioration of social injustice and in the improvement of physical, educational and cultural opportunity for the people that is patent to anyone whose memory goes back so far as a quarter of a century. But in regard to sexual conduct, and the vast social questions related thereto, we have not freed ourselves from the influence of primitive taboos. Even liberalism and rationalism has been asexualised. The early leaders of rationalist thought such as Godwin, Wolstonecraft and Shelley recognised that the reasoned attitude to life must be all embracing in its compass. Bradlaugh was the last popular leader to follow their path. After his time, and about the time that Ellis started working, radicalism and free-thought purchased an easy victory in the field of theological and political thought by hauling down its flag in the sexual and ethical field. Henceforward, the radical free-thinker, though he might deny the existence of God and proclaim that a beggar was as good as a king, could be relied on to behave exactly like an orthodox church-goer in his everyday life, or at least to accept the same hypocrisies and concealments. Such leaders of popular thought as Shaw and Wells were discreet and evasive when they came to deal with the sexual aspects of reform. If they advocated changes in sexual ethics the reform was

Above All Liberties

reserved, either explicitly or by implication, for some utopian future. The result of this tendency was that young men and women who grew up in the formative years of the present century became obsessed with the solution of economic and political problems as the means of ushering in the better world that was so confidently predicted by liberal prophets. The equally fundamental problems concerning population, eugenics, birth-control, marriage, the family, and sex education were side-tracked or, if considered at all, considered without subjecting the assumptions of orthodox opinion to the searching analysis which was breaking it down in other spheres. This unhealthy state of affairs may have contributed to the disappointments which the hopes of liberal idealism have since experienced. The world to-day might be a better place if the reformist and enthusiastic youth of the early twentieth century had read less Shaw and Wells and more Ellis.

Nevertheless Ellis's achievement has been great. His work impressed itself on the intelligentsia at an early date. So much so that in this country there was a marked cultural distinction between those sections of the community who had access to his work and to the works of the numerous Continental sexologists from whom he quoted, and the great mass of the public who had not that access. Ellis, for instance, was acquainted with Freud, from his earliest days, but Freud's books were not available in English till

Havelock Ellis

shortly before the last war. The great *Die Traumdeutung* published in 1900 was not translated till 1913. From the intelligentsia Ellis's ideas percolated slowly and belatedly to the general public. To-day they are doing much in all quarters to combat prejudice, ignorance and cruelty; and they have sweetened and ameliorated life for thousands. On the other hand orthodoxy still holds the fort so far as governmental and official expression of opinion is concerned. A House of Commons debate on any sexual subject is still the occasion for a mass display of ineptitude, ignorance and hypocrisy. During the first year of the present war the House devoted a long debate to decide the appellation proper to a soldier's wife in cases where there is no legal marriage. Indeed, the Labour Party are constantly distinguishing themselves by their inability to adopt an intelligent and progressive attitude to any problem in which a sexual factor is involved. This is probably due to the element of class distinction in the availability of sexual literature on which we shall have more to say presently. The law has only been changed grudgingly and in minor matters. It is still possible for judges and magistrates in their pontifications from the Bench to speak as if Ellis had never written. The abdication incident was an interesting example of herd reversion to primitive psychology.

But in spite of discouraging symptoms, I believe that the attitude of mind to sexual matters for which

Above All Liberties

Ellis stood is gaining ground among the masses of the people; and we must remember that it was to the encouragement of a civilised, rational and orderly attitude of mind rather than to the propagation of any specific doctrine that he devoted his life. It would be rash, however, to speak confidently of the future. It may be that the vision which inspired Ellis will be made actual, and that generations of free men and women will bless his name. It may be that the twilight of another dark age is gathering over Europe. In years to come some American Gibbon collecting material for a "Decline and Fall of Western Civilisation" may find reflected in Ellis's work all that was most promising and hopeful in that civilisation and in the neglect and persecution to which Ellis was subjected at a critical time, a contributory cause of the historical phenomenon he is studying.

CHAPTER V

THE STRANGE CASE OF COUNT POTOCKI OF MONTALK

THE ability of the London policeman to act as a general inquiry bureau in addition to carrying out his exacting duties has always evoked the admiration of visitors to the Metropolis. Country cousins, old ladies, foreigners with an inadequate command of English, and even small boys all receive courteous and efficient attention. Seldom has this omniscient service been put to a more surprising test than when two young men went up to a constable on duty outside the Old Bailey on January 13, 1932. They wanted to know where they could find a typesetter who would set up some spicy poems containing two of the most taboo words in the English language. Shakespeare makes play with the French equivalents of the words in question in the English lesson which Katherine receives prior to her marriage with Henry V. The constable did not appear to be shocked by their enunciation in plain English, and directed the inquirers to a nearby printing house. Either through ignorance or Puckishness on the policeman's part, this direction was not altogether satisfactory. The two prospective customers were politely bowed out with an apologetic "I'm afraid we couldn't undertake a job of that

Above All Liberties

sort, Sir," and the firm subsequently turned out to be the printers of the *Methodist Recorder*!

The two young men then continued light-heartedly on their way to find a more accommodating establishment. Before following them further, however, it would be well to make their closer acquaintance. One, Mr. Douglas Glass, need not detain us as he soon passes from the stage of the tragi-comedy of which these seemingly trivial incidents were the prelude. His companion, however, was the protagonist of the drama—Count Geoffrey Wladislac Vaile Potocki of Montalk. He wore a voluminous wine-red cloak and leather sandals, while his long hair fell over his shoulders. These personal details are worthy of notice because they have a bearing on his subsequent misfortunes. His appearance (which remains unchanged to-day) could only create prejudice in the drab surroundings of modern London and in the grey minds of its rulers. His opinions are as remarkable as his apparel. Born in New Zealand, the son of an architect and the grandson of a Polish professor, he was educated for the law but deserted it to assert his claims to be a poet by divine right and King of Poland by heredity. Proclaiming himself pagan by religion, he has, since 1936, edited and produced a periodical called *The Right Review* which maintains a Royalist, anti-democratic position of the most extreme kind. Like many another aspirant who has left the safe ways of bourgeois life in search of literary and other fame,

The Strange Case of Count Potocki of Montalk

Count Potocki has experienced poverty and neglect. But let him state his main thesis in his own words, taken from a book of poems entitled *Surprising Songs* published two years before the incidents here narrated:

> . . . For a loving race, children of a new dawn,
>
> consecrate before the angelic hosts
> among the heights of heaven, before my birth,
> I was annointed by the gods that rule the earth,
> . . . True I have been wrecked on terrestrial coasts,
>
> wandered unknown among an alien folk
> who could not see my invisible robe of dreams,
> but my people know me by my sceptre's gleams,
> and by my sea-blue eyes. They love their yoke
>
> for the mild decrees to which I set my hand
> are always, that they shall love the lovable,
> and the very footsteps of the beautiful,
> and they obey, the people of my land.

At the end of their quest the Count and Mr. Glass found themselves in conversation with a Mr. de Lozey, the manager of a firm of linotype operators. The Count produced the manuscript of five short poems which he wished to have set up in linotype so that he could print copies on a hand press at home for circulation among his friends. Mr. de Lozey examined the manuscript and said that the price would be 25s. The Count considered this too high. The dis-

Above All Liberties

cussion seems to have broadened to a consideration of *Lady Chatterley's Lover* and *Ulysses*, on the merits of which Mr. Glass delivered himself at some length, and added some expressions of anti-semitic opinion. The manager did not appear at all shocked but he seems to have become annoyed. In the end it was arranged that the manuscript should be left with him and that the Count would return with the money if he could not get the job done cheaper elsewhere. He and Mr. Glass then left the place.

The next thing they knew of the affair was that they were both arrested and thrown into Brixton prison. The manager had shown the manuscript to the police after his prospective customers had gone.

Now what of this manuscript? I have already indicated that it contained words that, though used by Chaucer and other masters of English, had fallen out of decent literary usage until the recent efforts of Lawrence and Joyce to restore them to respectability. But a rather closer examination is necessary to appreciate the subsequent development of this case. This examination is possible because the manuscript was pirated during the proceedings and unauthorised copies are by no means uncommon.

Of the five poems, the last is easiest to dispose of. It is a translation of Rabelais' "Chanson de la Braguette." Urquhart's unvarnished rendering of this little pleasantry into seventeenth-century English can be obtained in any bookshop for a couple of shillings.

The Strange Case of Count Potocki of Montalk

I think Montalk's version an improvement on Urquhart because it retains the metre and rime pattern of the original. The fourth poem, entitled "In the Manner of Paul Verlaine, Roman Catholic Poet," is a parody or free translation of Verlaine's "Idylle High Life" which begins *"La galopine à la pleine main. . . ."* Montalk's version seems to me to capture something of the sparkling (and grossly improper) gaiety of the French. The poem comes from *Femmes,* one of the three collections of erotic verse published by Verlaine *"sous le manteau."* The other two are *Amies* and *Hombres.* Most editions of these collections appeared under Verlaine's pseudonym: Pablo de Herlagnez. When the Montalk's little pamphlet came into the august presence of the Court of Criminal Appeal, as it ultimately did, Mr. Justice Acton, one of the judges, said that he read Verlaine himself and the poet never wrote anything like this alleged translation. In his *ex parte* account of the proceedings, published under the title *Whited Sepulchres,* Montalk makes great play with his Lordship's ignorance without mentioning the surreptitious nature of the publication of "Idylle High Life." This is hardly fair, since one could read the whole of Verlaine in the collected edition of his works without knowing that this poem existed. On the other hand, Verlaine's erotic trilogy was freely discussed and quoted from in a French biography published in 1929 and translated into English during the year of the trial.

Above All Liberties

A knowledge of it is necessary for a complete understanding of Verlaine's mind and for a full appreciation of some of his other poetry. Montalk's poem was sub-headed "An ode to the Blessed Virgin Mary is understood on the opposite page." This is presumably intended to emphasise the dual nature of Verlaine's character, but it should be noted that his beautiful religious verse (written in rare intervals of piety when absinthe was scarce or unobtainable) was never mixed up with the erotic trilogy. This small matter is worth mentioning because Montalk has been inclined to attribute the ferocity of the proceedings against him to Roman Catholic persecution.

The two poems we have dealt with take up forty-five of the total of the sixty-three lines contained in the brochure. So far it can be said that the brochure, although not everyone's meat, could be of legitimate interest to anyone whose tastes were literary without being prudish. Neither Rabelais's vigour nor Verlaine's delicate mastery of French verse are in any way diminished even when they deal with subject matter normally found repulsive.

The remaining eighteen lines of the brochure make up a poem, "For — and his girl, on leaving them the key of my room," and two other short original pieces. It must suffice to say that these are in the same vein as the translation of Rabelais and the parody of Verlaine, and by that token quite unsuitable for polite society in twentieth-century England. But it must be remem-

The Strange Case of Count Potocki of Montalk

bered that Montalk did not intend the brochure for general publication but for private circulation among his friends whose literary tastes presumably were similar to his own. That such tastes are by no means unusual among literary people is evidenced by the vogue of *Ulysses*. There is hardly a post-war writer in English whose style has not been influenced by this masterpiece, and it has been praised by critics of the highest standing. Beside this mountain of obscenity (now openly sold in the streets of London) the Count's brochure is a mole-hill as much as regards degree as quantity. Furthermore, it is worthy of note that since Montalk's case two editions of the *Canterbury Tales*, in which Chaucer's broad stories and language are no longer, as formerly, veiled in Middle English, have freely circulated in Great Britain.

As soon as Montalk and Mr. Glass were in Brixton Prison they found what a net of difficulties enmeshes anyone who falls foul of the law. Although in theory "an accused person is innocent until proved guilty," his lot is far from happy. It would have been easy for both prisoners to have found bail, but they were not allowed to use the telephone. Furthermore, their friends could not 'phone them because the number of Brixton Prison is not in the Directory and cannot be obtained on inquiry. One humorous episode, however, enlivened the Count's captivity. His celebrated cloak was taken away from him. He demanded it back, and ended with an interview with the

Above All Liberties

Governor. The Governor decided that, as unconvicted prisoners are entitled to their own clothes, he had no power to withhold the cloak. It was therefore returned to its owner, who wore it by day and used it as an extra blanket against the cold January weather at night.

On the third day Montalk's brother was successful in getting him bailed, and Montalk set about performing a similar service for Mr. Glass. The case came before the Clerkenwell Police Court. Mr. de Lozey in the witness-box was very strong on his moral scruples. He said that he would certainly inform if he were offered an obscene Greek manuscript to print. He looked rather foolish when he had to admit that he knew no Greek. The Magistrate seemed to take a reasonable view of the case. The Count, however, was very angry and indignant at what he considered to be wrongful arrest, and insisted on trial by jury. His bail was renewed, and Mr. Glass was discharged from the proceedings on the ground that no jury would convict him.

The trial came on at the Old Bailey on February 8th. The judge was the Recorder of London, Sir Ernest Wild. If Count Potocki was the protagonist of this little drama, Sir Ernest was the deuteragonist. It would simplify this story if I could represent him to the reader as a sort of modern and petty Judge Jefferies. But, in the first place, this would not be true; and, in the second, it would detract from the significance of

The Strange Case of Count Potocki of Montalk

the story. It is just because Sir Ernest Wild was an able, distinguished and respected member of the Judiciary, noted for his practical kindness to the criminals with whom he came in touch, that the case he tried on that day in 1932 is so important. Because he was typical rather than exceptional his attitude to, and conduct of, the case have far-reaching implications. Born in 1869, Ernest Wild graduated at Jesus College, Cambridge, in 1890 and was called to the Bar in 1893. At the astonishingly early age of twenty-eight he was appointed Judge of a local Court at Norwich—the youngest judge who ever presided over an English Court. His judicial duties did not prevent him subsequently sitting on the London County Council and afterwards becoming a Conservative Member of Parliament. In 1922 he was made Recorder of London, which appointment he held until his death in 1934. His biography by Robert J. Blackham is a long adulatory chronicle of a career which, while rising above professional mediocrity, never approached brilliance. Sir Ernest was a great speaker, always saying the right thing at the right moment, and throughout a long life he seems to have eschewed any appearance of wrongdoing or unconventionality. In short, Sir Ernest Wild was a typical member of the English governing class of to-day: as ordinary, respectable, and unimaginative as Count Potocki of Montalk is extraordinary, unconventional and poetic.

Before the trial began the Recorder told three

Above All Liberties

women who had been balloted for the jury that it was a very "filthy" case. He made use of this and similar expressions several times during the trial. The women were informed that they need not serve and two retired, but the third firmly declined to do so. Now the only point at issue in the trial was whether the poems were, in the circumstances of their publication, "obscene"; and this question of "obscenity" is one of fact for the jury. Surely, then, it was one on which the judge should not express bias either way. What would be thought if, in a trial in which the whole point at issue was whether the defendant had committed murder, manslaughter, or justifiable homicide, the judge consistently referred to accused's "murderous" conduct?

Count Potocki has produced a considerable volume of lyric poetry which has received high praise from competent critics. Some of it has appeared in periodicals of the standing of *Country Life*. The Recorder was furnished at the trial with copies of his published collections: *Wild Oats* (1927), *Surprising Songs* (1930) and *Lordly Lovesongs* (1931). But he paid little attention to them.

There was little dispute as to the facts of the case against the Count. The prosecution had to prove that the character of the poems was such that their "publication" in the admitted circumstances was a criminal offence.

In his summing-up the Recorder betrayed his own

opinion in an unmistakable fashion. "Are you going to allow a man, because he calls himself a poet, to deflower our English language by popularising these words?" he asked, and continued, "Remember the standard of morals has advanced. It used to be," etc. Sir Ernest apparently held the curious, but not uncommon, view that the prudery which distinguished the comparatively short and quite exceptional period of English history from the death of Smollett to the last war was somehow an "advance" on what had gone before and in the nature of a permanent, rather than a temporary, addition to the national culture. At another point in the summing-up the Recorder said: "A man must not say he is a poet and be filthy. He has to obey the law just the same as ordinary citizens, and the sooner the highbrow school learns that the better for the morality of the country."

In spite of this very one-sided summing-up, the jury were some time considering their verdict, and wished to retire from the box, but the Recorder prevailed upon them to stay where they were. At last the foreman came forward and those in the Court formed the opinion that he would have given a qualified verdict had not the Recorder interrupted him. Anyhow a verdict of "Guilty" was entered to the satisfaction of the Recorder, who observed: "No decent-minded jury could have come to any other decision than that the defendant had attempted to deprave our literature."

Above All Liberties

It is important to observe that in the remarks quoted the judge sets himself up not only as a judge of law but of literature, and as a sort of protector of English literature from the "depraving" effects of writers whose tastes were other than his own. We are therefore entitled to inquire into Sir Ernest's qualifications for this task. Fortunately (for this inquiry) he published a volume of verse of his own composition in 1919 entitled *The Lamp of Destiny and other Poems* which throws a great deal of light on his claim to be an arbiter of literary taste.

One short poem from its sixty-odd pages is a fair sample of the whole:

REFLECTIONS

I watched the Sun a-sinking
    In the sea;
And oh! I fell a-thinking
    All of thee.
And oh! I fell a-thinking
His radiant beauty drinking,
Just as the Sun was sinking
    In the sea.

I saw the Sun reflected
    For a space;
His beams, Sweetheart, directed
    On thy face.
His beams to thee directed
As if he recollected
'Twas good to be reflected
    On thy face.

The Strange Case of Count Potocki of Montalk

Many of us have written this sort of thing in adolescence. But to *publish* it at the mature age of fifty-nine argues a state of arrested emotional development or a depravity of poetic taste both equally remarkable. The volume contains an inevitable war poem in which the bellicose patriotism often expressed by those over military age in 1914 is given full rein. The German armies are "Satan's legions." Of the religious sentiment liberally dispersed throughout the book I am unqualified to form an opinion; but the not unexpected parade of Classical learning seems a little odd from one to whose cheek the sexual customs of centuries of Graeco-Roman civilisation would have brought one long blush.[1] Altogether, this book is a little compendium of commonplace thought put into puerile verse in which the "poetic diction" of the Victorian

[1] A heavy proportion of criminals find it a paying profession to solicit homosexual addicts in the streets of London and then to demand money from them on threat of exposure. Most of the victims submit to the blackmail levy, for although theoretically the police are supposed to prosecute on blackmail charges without making inquiries as to the character of the injured person, the homosexual fears that actually inquiries will be made and that he will be placed on the list of police suspects. The late Sir Ernest Wild unconsciously abetted this evil by insisting on calling the victim into open court and asking him a number of searching questions. He did so apparently on account of his detestation of homosexuality, and was indeed so obsessed by this detestation that he would always arrange for blackmail charges of this type to be heard before himself, the natural result being that such victims dared not face the ordeal and dared not therefore prosecute. Sir Ernest Wild was accordingly known among London criminals as the "blackmailer's friend."—*Sex-morality Tomorrow*, by Kenneth Ingram (London, 1940).

Above All Liberties

era is studiously followed. The *Times* obituary discreetly suppressed the fact of this literary indiscretion. Having been forced to bring it to light, I cannot resist the temptation to refer to one more gem from the collection. In an item entitled "The Toy of Fate," "Tenor" sings the praises of his fair-haired lady-love, the "Bass" exalts one whose tresses are "black as the raven's wing," finally both combine in the following duet:

> Impotent men we,
> Impotent when we,
> Stricken by Cupid's dart,
> Wake to discover
> Each is a lover
> Of some quick-beating heart. . . .

I am not sure that Count Potocki was not in some degree the victim of law reform. Before the Indictments Act of 1915, the indictment in obscene libel cases was worded thus:

that (so-and-so) being a person of a wicked and depraved mind and disposition, and unlawfully and wickedly devising, contriving, and intending, to vitiate and corrupt the morals of the liege subjects of our said Lord the King, to debauch and poison the minds of divers of the liege subjects of our said Lord the King, and to raise and create in them lustful desires, and to bring the said liege subjects into a state of wickedness, lewdness and debauchery, on the ...... day of ......, in the year of our Lord, etc., and within the jurisdiction of the said Court, unlawfully, wickedly, maliciously, scandalously, and wilfully did

The Strange Case of Count Potocki of Montalk

publish, etc., a certain lewd, wicked, bawdy, scandalous, and obscene libel, in the form of a book entitled .... in which said book are contained among other things, divers wicked, lewd, impure, scandalous and obscene libels. . . . To the manifest corruption of the morals and minds of the liege subjects of our said Lord the King, in contempt of our said Lord the King, and his laws, in violation of common decency, morality, and good order, and against the peace of our said Lord the King, his Crown and Dignity.

I scarcely think that even Sir Ernest Wild could have persuaded a jury that Montalk was guilty of this dreadful crime. There is a suggestion of public and widespread disturbance of a sensational nature. The Indictments Act of 1915 did away with this picturesque phraseology in regard to obscene libel and many other matters. The charge is now simply that of having "published an obscene libel." The purpose of the Act was to save time and trouble, and it did not in any way alter the offence; but it is now open to a judge to explain to a bewildered jury that the cryptic words "publishing an obscene libel" can cover a communication made to one other party only and which has done no harm to anyone. It was this last interpretation of the law that enabled Sir Archibald Bodkin, as Director of Public Prosecutions, to boast before the International Conference for the Suppression of Obscene Publications at Geneva in 1923, that he had got two people in prison for merely exchanging obscene matter between themselves.

Above All Liberties

Montalk having been convicted, the usual police evidence of character was called for. It is a serious blemish on British justice that on these occasions the police are allowed to report any unproven tittle-tattle about the convicted person. It is, of course, proper that in passing sentence a judge should be guided by a man's previous record, but fairness demands that the account given should be confined to a bare recital of previous convictions, if any. But, on the contrary, the police make all sorts of vague and irrelevant statements to the accused's prejudice such as "he is a Communist," "an agitator," "drinks," "lives in sin," etc. Count Potocki had a perfectly clean record, but a police officer went into the witness-box to say (*a*) that a copy of *The Well of Loneliness* was found in his rooms and (*b*) that "the young woman living with the accused was the daughter of highly respectable parents who had tried to get her back." With regard to the first point, it would be interesting to know why the Count should not have possessed a book of which over a hundred thousand copies have been sold and which has been translated into many foreign languages. The second point only deserved to be treated as gossip.

During the trial Montalk's indignation at what he considered the injustice of the whole proceedings continued to rise. He refused to make any statement in mitigation of sentence, and the Recorder asked him, "Can't you suggest what punishment you think

The Strange Case of Count Potocki of Montalk

you deserve?" "Yes, my Lord!" replied the infuriated Count, "I think I deserve to be sentenced to several years in Buckingham Palace!" He was, in fact, sentenced to *six months'* imprisonment in the second division. W. B. Yeats, the Irish poet, subsequently described this imprisonment as "criminally brutal." Common sense suggests that a small fine and an admonition to be more careful in future would have satisfied the harshest rigour of the law.

At this point Sir Ernest Wild passes from the scene. He died a few years after the trial. It is interesting to note in passing that two other occupants of the Bench involved in the obscenity trials we have noticed did not long survive the judgments which have made them notorious. Sir Charles Hall died in the prime of life just after the Bedborough case, and Sir Percival Clarke was dead within a year of condemning *The Sexual Impulse.* Many insignificant persons, clothed with a little judicial authority, have acquired an unenviable immortality because they have been unable to recognise greatness when it swam into their mundane ken. We remember Sir Charles Hall only because he was unable to distinguish between Havelock Ellis and a common pornographer, Sir George Jessel because he insulted Annie Besant, Lord Eldon because of his foolish ideas about Shelley's poetry. We may be fairly confident that posterity will consign *The Lamp of Destiny* to a merciful oblivion, but its author may be remembered because he did less than

Above All Liberties

justice to a man who, by the severest judgment, was no more than a harmless crank, and who may turn out to be a genius.

An appeal fund was raised and subscriptions came in from all quarters. Among the subscribers were Aldous Huxley, H. G. Wells, J. B. Priestley, Walter de la Mare, Laurence Housman, Lord Esher, T. S. Eliot and Hugh Walpole. The appeal was heard on March 7th. The Count had spent the intervening time in prison. Appellants to the Court of Criminal Appeal who have not obtained bail pending appeal suffer considerable disabilities. For one thing the lowering effects of prison diet make it very difficult for them to give a good account of themselves unless friends outside send a dinner in to them on the day of the trial. This was not done in the Count's case, and there is no doubt that he made a poor showing. So far as he was concerned the appeal was a complete failure. The unlucky prisoner could only console himself with the fact that the case went some way to establishing that in "obscene libel" cases:

it is a good defence to the charge that the publication of matter prima facie obscene was for the public good, as being necessary or advantageous to religion, science, literature or art, provided that the manner and extent of the publication does not exceed what the public good requires.

Even if this very cautious piece of reasonableness be taken as established law, Montalk's case shows the situation to be about as unsatisfactory as it can

The Strange Case of Count Potocki of Montalk

be. The law claims, and successfully claims, to arraign writers before the bar of justice to answer for questions of taste. And this not only in respect of published works but in respect of work passed among themselves and their friends. The standard of taste is to be that which appeals to the aged occupants of the judicial bench. On this basis some of the most important living moulders of English literature could be made criminals. Sir Ernest Wild was quite clear that he would like to have made them so. To believe that this challenge by the law to literature can be ultimately successful is to believe that artistic taste can be forced into a static mould and that the pen is not a creative and evolving force but an instrument to be prostituted to the perpetuation of things as they are. Experience since Montalk's imprisonment suggests that the challenge will not be ultimately successful. Neither James Joyce, nor the publishers of Chaucer in modern dress, have been attacked, although they have used in public precisely the same words as those for which Montalk was punished for using in private.

In the short run, however, the law rode rough-shod over its victim. He served his sentence and the account he gave of his sufferings under the title *Snobbery with Violence* commends him to the sympathy of any humane person. Prison reform has gone to such a length that it is possible that brutal criminals are (to use the words of reactionaries) "treated better than they deserve." But for the better class of prisoner,

Above All Liberties

and particularly for a man of refinement, an English prison is still a purgatory. It may seem a little thing not to be able to cut one's finger nails, but even so robust a prisoner as Benevenuto Cellini complains of this matter:

> My nails only which had grown gave me great distress; for I could not touch myself without wounding myself with them: I could not dress myself because they turned inwards or outwards giving me such pain. (*Life*, Bk. II, Ch. 25.)

Again, Montalk found that it was in practice impossible to visit a water-closet after 4.30 in the afternoon. Food in prison is bad, and upsets anyone used to a healthy diet. Its high starch content combined with the relative inactivity of prison life, however, causes the prisoner to put on weight, and this is cynically pointed to as evidence of its adequacy. Furthermore, all prisoners suspect that the food is doped with bromide in order to reduce sexual stimulation. But over and above everything, for the literary man, loom the senseless restrictions on reading and writing. The English prison regulations of to-day had they existed in the past, would have prevented the production of such literary masterpieces as Bunyan's *Pilgrim's Progress*.

The Count, I for one am pleased to note, did not take the treatment to which he was subjected in a spirit of meek resignation. His *Whited Sepulchres* is a vociferous, and by no means temperate, protest

The Strange Case of Count Potocki of Montalk

against the injustice he experienced. I am glad of it. I see no reason why the victims of injustice should be polite and mealy-mouthed to their oppressors. It is interesting to note, however, that he is less bitter against the authorities than against the lawyers who defended him, and less bitter against them than against the Left-wing notables who organised his defence. So far as the lawyers are concerned I think he is entirely wrong. It is useless to put up any intelligent argument on a question of sexual morals in an English Court of Law. Any attempt to state the Count's case as he saw it himself would probably have brought even worse disasters upon him; and, considering his own intransigence, it is probable that his advocates did as well for him as anyone could. His animosity against his Left-wing supporters is more interesting. I know nothing of the personalities involved, but I can well believe that the Count found much to infuriate him. There is to-day among some of those who are most loud in their concern for English liberty a hesitancy when it comes to the practical application of principles, a preoccupation with their own respectability, an anxiety to be sure that they are on "a good case," a puritanical attitude to sexual matters and even a slight flavour of humbug. Some experience of this may well have proved intensely irritating to one so far removed from the orbit of the work-a-day world as Count Potocki. Liberalism in England to-day seems to have shed many of the virtues derived from its Puritan origin without divesting itself of the corresponding disabilities. A firmer, more consistent, more comprehensive, and more militant attitude in the face of reaction is necessary if such cases as that of Montalk are not to be repeated.

CHAPTER VI

THE WIDER CENSORSHIP

THE deprivation which the community suffers as a result of the law of "obscene libel" cannot be measured by the list of judicial condemnations. First of all there is the effect of apprehension of an arbitrary and unpredictable law on authors. Mr. Cyril Connolly, a critic and man of letters of high repute, considered it advisable to publish his novel *The Rock Pool* (1936) in France, although the story, a study of English and American life in the South of France, is no more outspoken than many novels which escape attack in this country. A number of American novels have been published in Paris rather than London for the same reason. Even if the author has the courage of his convictions, his publisher may demur against taking risks. How much restraint comes from this quarter no one will ever know. But in America, Floyd Dell's *Janet March* (1923) was withdrawn for a time at the publisher's instance; and Theodore Dreiser's *Sister Carrie* (1900) was temporarily suppressed by his publishers, it is said because of a protest by one of the Doubleday ladies. Although the firm were under contract to publish they printed only a few copies, and sold less. Lionel Britton's novel *Hunger and Love* (although freely circulated in this country) has never been re-

Above All Liberties

leased for sale in the States, and an edition printed in 1931 has been shunted from publisher to publisher. Britton's frank and realistic treatment of the life of a London errand boy, because it does not omit his sexual frustrations and struggles, raises fears of prosecution for "obscenity."

Again the law places an intolerable burden on the printer, who cannot be expected to share the enthusiasms of either author or publisher, although he is equally responsible with them in law. He may be forgiven if, from time to time, he plays for safety in a rather uninstructed way. Finally, there are the difficulties of the distributing agents. They are mostly concerned with periodicals and newspapers. Their difficulties are most acute in respect of foreign importations. For instance, in 1937 (*Times*, February 3rd) Henri Bonnaire, an agent for a large number of the most reputable art and literary societies in France, was before the Lewes Police Court. A number of magazines imported by him from Paris had been seized by the Customs. The Court ordered the magazines to be destroyed. Agents who deal in great quantities of periodical literature are scarcely in a position to examine closely everything they sell, and their position is perhaps more inequitable than that of any other parties to literary transactions. It is therefore not surprising that in 1939 a Conference of the National Federation of Retail Newsagents, Booksellers and Stationers unanimously endorsed a pro-

The Wider Censorship

posal that a "Board of Censors," on the lines of the film censorship, was needed to deal with obscene literature. The proposal, although understandable on the part of a body of woefully harassed tradesmen, was, of course, entirely reactionary in its nature, and its adoption would have involved all the evils and absurdities of literary censorship in the true sense of the term.

The nervousness and conservatism of the distributing trade has been a considerable handicap to the nudist movement as regards its illustrated publications. Photographs of sunbathing camps and of nudist activities are of legitimate interest to adherents to the movement. Many nudist magazines published abroad contain interesting and tasteful pictures in which what is known as integral nudism plays a part. At one time the authorities here took the line that any illustration in which pubic hair was visible was necessarily "obscene" in law. But this interpretation of the law seems to have gone by the board. A reproduction of a naturalistic modern German painting of the nude appeared in the *Listener* for September 22, 1937. Prosecutions in respect of integral pictures in nudist magazines have been unsuccessful, notably that of an American sunbathing magazine, the *Nudist*, in Cornwall in the following May. Subsequently in September 1938 a Bond Street photographer successfully appealed at London Sessions against a fine imposed by Mr. J. B. Sandbach, K.C., at Marlborough

Above All Liberties

Street Police Court in respect of the sale of photographs of artists' models. It seems clear that naturalistic nudity in itself does not constitute "obscenity" so long as the picture or illustration is in other ways indubitably decent. Nevertheless English sunbathing magazines continue to observe a tradition of careful posing and, where this fails to produce the required concealment, retouching is resorted to. I understand that this is largely due to the susceptibilities of the distributing trade. In relation to pictorial "obscenity" we may notice that in the last century the English Customs authorities destroyed a set of pictures which Boucher executed for the Pompadour. Louis XVI had them removed from the Arsenal palace with the command: *Il faut faire disparaître ces indécences*; nevertheless they were of undoubted historical and artistic interest.

We see that the influence of a relatively few legal condemnations spreads like the rings on water into which a stone has been dropped. Another important factor is the influence of the libraries. For decades Mudies exercised a censorship that far outran anything necessitated by the law. That venerable firm, however, came to an end in 1937, and the up-to-date subscription libraries tend to be more liberal. This can hardly be said in regard to libraries supported out of the rates. A most remarkable example of the obscurantist attitude adopted by the bodies who control these libraries was brought to light by Dr. W. A. Brend in

The Wider Censorship

a letter to the *Freethinker* of February 7, 1937. Dr. Brend wrote:

You were kind enough to review my book, *Sacrifice to Attis: A study of sex and civilisation*, at some length in the *Freethinker* last autumn. In view of the appeal of the London Labour Party for the support of those with progressive ideas at the forthcoming L.C.C. election, it may interest you to know that the Council has decided that my book is "unsuitable" for their Education Library—a library, I understand, intended mainly for the use of teachers.

Dr. Brend is an eminent neurologist whose experience with war pensioners has given him a unique insight into the sexual and home difficulties of the very people whose children are put in charge of London County Council teachers. It may seem surprising that a Labour Education Committee should behave in this way, but it is a mistake to suppose that the Labour Party is distinguished for liberalism in these matters. Indeed, when any sexual subject is raised in the House of Commons what little sense is talked always comes from the Conservative benches.

This may to some extent be due to the sharp class division which the law has created so far as sexual knowledge and access to sexual literature is concerned. Only the privileged classes can obtain really plain-spoken books on sex and read foreign and classical works which bear on the subject.

For one thing, a high price often shields a book from attack, while a low price sometimes seems to

Above All Liberties

invite prosecution. At one time even so liberal a thinker as H. G. Wells favoured[1] this very undemocratic arrangement. How the system works is well illustrated by the example of James Hanley's *Boy*. The novel is a study of the sufferings of a working lad who runs away to sea because he finds conditions at home intolerable. As his sexual troubles were dealt with in an open and sincere way, the publishers only dared to print the manuscript as written in a very limited edition at two guineas. In the ordinary edition, published in 1931 at 7s. 6d., certain passages and words were replaced by asterisks after the method employed in the English edition of Richard Aldington's *Death of a Hero*. Later, on the advice of D. H. Lawrence, the asterisks were replaced by some "innocuous" writing. All was well until, after two reprints, a cheap edition at 3s. 6d. was issued in 1934. Then the publishers were prosecuted and the book suppressed.

Then it will be remembered that when *The Sexual Impulse* was banned the magistrate asked Janet Chance, who gave evidence that the book was in the library at her Sex Education Centre: "Have you ever given the book to a member of the working class?" The need for explicit books of sex instruction at popular prices is clear from a perusal of the most widely read work on this subject. I have nothing but

[1] See *Christianity and Sex Problems*, by Hugh Northcote (Philadelphia, 1916), 2nd edition, p. 2.

The Wider Censorship

admiration for the skill and pertinacity with which Dr. Stopes has got over to a wide audience the maximum amount of sex education possible at the dates of publication of her various books. But a glance at the passages in *Married Love* and *Enduring Passion* dealing with coital technique and impotence will show the extent of the reticence and inexplicitness which prevailing prudery appears to have forced upon the author. When we remember that these books are not cheap and that, in spite of their almost fanatical advocacy of monogamy, they are rarely obtainable at the public libraries, we realise how deep is the ignorance in which the average worker finds himself in regard to fact and speculation on sexual matters.

It is in the running of the public libraries, on which the masses rely for so much of their reading matter, that this class bias is most clearly in evidence. The committees in control of many of these libraries, as a matter of policy, refuse to buy important books with a wide circulation among those who can afford to buy books or join subscription libraries. Of course, a library dependent on a limited allocation from the rates cannot buy every important book that is published, but some committees use the discretion forced on them by limited means to discriminate against books that are considered unorthodox, especially in the sexual spheres. Too often the qualifications of the local councillors in whose hands the task of selection is placed do not extend beyond prejudice and sus-

Above All Liberties

ceptibility to "public opinion" as evidenced by the complaints of local busybodies. The question of their suitability for their task is becoming one of increasing importance. More and more public money is being spent on these libraries. Those who are willing to co-operate are being organised on a national basis under a splendid scheme which culminates in the National Central Library. Very soon it should be possible for anyone who can pay the necessary postage to borrow from any public library in England besides drawing on a reserve of 135,000 volumes held by the National Central Library, and a further 6,500,000 volumes at call in "outlier" libraries who are ready to lend to the National Central Library. The policy of the National Central Library is not questioned, but clearly it leans very heavily on the local libraries and the value of its work depends to a large extent on local selection providing a fair and scholarly representation of extant literature.

Some librarians are rather complacent on this subject. The Report of the Librarian of a London borough for 1937 states: "In St. Pancras we have had very little trouble over such matters," and continues to say that books are chosen "largely on the basis of a uniformly good reception at the hands of acknowledged critics, or by reason of the status of the writers." So far so good. But we also learn that "members of the reading public exercise a censorship of their own. Our practice is to withdraw a book from general

The Wider Censorship

circulation after it has been objected to three times. Such books are shelved away from the public departments." One does not wish to underrate the literary ability of the ratepayers of St. Pancras, but surely it is somewhat *over*-rated when any three of them can overrule the voice of acknowledged critics or the judgment of writers of status.

The system of withdrawing books from the open shelves of public libraries in this way is very widespread. A few years ago the town of Bootle was convulsed by a controversy caused by the local Town Council placing Richard Aldington's *Death of a Hero* on the reserved shelves of its Public Library after it had been on the open shelves for over six years. The action meant that henceforth a visit to his public library would not enlighten the Bootle townsman as to the existence of Mr. Aldington's novel. He would only be able to borrow it if, already knowing of its existence and its presence in the library, he made a special demand for it. In this case the Bootle Corporation did little more than offer a gratuitous and totally unjustifiable affront to a writer of eminence. The townsfolk were quick to find out that the novel (of which most of them had probably never heard) could be obtained for sixpence, and the local booksellers were soon sold out! This incident may have inspired a very amusing broadcast on local library censorship in the "Burbleton" series in 1938.

This system has, however, serious consequences.

Above All Liberties

Since only reactionaries seek to combat supposed errors in ethics or taste by suppression it means that the open shelves of the public libraries present a false and one-sided impression of the attitude taken by the literary world on questions on which public opinion is sharply divided.

But one example is worth a string of generalities. In Hampstead the rates support a Public Library of some hundred thousand volumes. So far as literature with any sexual bearing is concerned, it is run on parish pump lines by people who esteem it their main duty "to protect the morals of Hampstead." There is on the public shelves a book which, under a spurious guise of broad-mindedness and modernity now becoming fashionable in certain religious quarters, puts forward a completely unscientific view in regard to masturbation. This view in its milder forms may well give a twist to the mind of a growing lad, which, if uncorrected, will incapacitate him for happy marriage and useful citizenship in after-life. In its more extreme form it actually drove a London boy to suicide not long ago. If there ever was an "immoral" book I regard this as one.

But neither I nor any other modernist would agitate for its suppression under the "reserve shelf" system which operates at Hampstead. I only deny the right of reactionaries to relegate books expounding more scientific views (such as my *Sex and Revolution*) to the reserve closet. A young person coming to a public

The Wider Censorship

library to enlighten himself on questions of doubt and difficulty (as he has a right to do) should find on the public shelves (as he will expect to find) a fair representation of the varying opinions on the matter.

One can have a certain amount of sympathy with the harassed librarian in view of the nuisance value of the prurient Puritan, but if he is driven to adopt this system its unfair results could be avoided at least so far as works of non-fiction are concerned. If the system is, in fact, justifiable it should be applied without discrimination to *all* books on sex. As things are at present it is only the works of writers like Bertrand Russell which go into the reserve closet. Attacks on their line of thought, e.g. *The New Morality* by G. E. Newsom (1932) and other works of the orthodox are allowed on the public shelves.

One final legal point is perhaps worthy of mention. Insurance policies are unenforceable in so far as they cover "obscene" matter. Considering how numerous and various are the books which have been held to be legally obscene this point is of some importance to librarians and owners of private collections. The difficulty can only be overcome by a "gentleman's agreement" with the insurance company that in the event of a claim they will not raise the issue of "obscenity." Not long ago one of the leading London insurance companies not only refused to enter into such an understanding, but stated that in dealing with fire claims in respect of books their assessors looked

Above All Liberties

out for evidence of "obscenity" and the company's practice was to repudiate that part of their contract found to cover "obscene" matter.

To appreciate the importance of the wide repercussions of the law of obscene libel which we have been considering, we must remember that liberal culture is threatened in all parts of the world to-day. It can only be firmly rooted where new books which contain the nascent thought of the community are available for everyone who can profit by them irrespective of his economic or social position; and where the facilities for research necessary to serious authorship are open to all. The National Central Library is working towards the first part of this ideal. The British Museum should go a long way towards fulfilling the second. Unfortunately the evening opening of the Reading Room was suspended as a measure of economy during the war of 1914–18 and never fully restored. For twenty years the Reading Room shut at six o'clock, the very hour at which those employed during the day might make use of it. The contribution to scholarship and letters by this class of person in the past should surely warrant them better treatment. In 1937 the hour was extended to seven o'clock, but it is to be hoped that, when the restrictions due to the present war are no longer necessary, the full evening opening will be restored.

The importance of making literature free from all shackles legal, economic and social is enhanced by the

The Wider Censorship

way in which other avenues of cultural expression are closed to ideas which do not appeal to the aged and the orthodox. The stage censorship has hampered every attempted advance in the English theatre, and Bernard Shaw has waged a lifelong war against it. The newer forms of expression are even worse. The narrowness of the film censorship and the ineptitude of the British Board of Film Censors has been exposed by Ivor Montagu in *The Political Censorship of Films* (1929). The B.B.C., from which so much might have been expected, was subjected during its formative decade to an astonishing regime of combined militarism and clericalism, as witness Mr. R. S. Lambert, editor of the *Listener* from 1929–39, in his *Ariel and all his Quality* (1940).

The official reason given for censorship of all kinds is that the institution concerned cannot advance ahead of public opinion. But public opinion in so far as it is vital is created by pioneers who are able to think and act free of official supervision. If the present tendency continues and cultural institutions and resources are taken more and more out of private hands the official sheep will soon have no wetherbell to follow. The maintenance of truly liberal conditions in at least one sphere of intellectual and creative expression is therefore essential to the continuance of civilisation as we know it.

CHAPTER VII

TO BEG I AM ASHAMED

An undesirable feature of the uncertainties and absurdities of the law of obscene libel deserves special treatment, namely the way in which they lend themselves to exploitation by the press. It is well known that the foolish prosecution of *The Well of Loneliness* followed an attack in the *Sunday Express* by the late Mr. James Douglas, in which he made the astonishing statement that he would rather put a phial of prussic acid into the hands of a healthy girl or boy than Miss Radclyffe Hall's novel.

On January 16, 1937, the same distinguished journalist in an article headed "This book *must* be banned" informed the readers of the *Daily Express* that a novel recently published by the old and respected firm of Dent was "poison gas" and made him "choke and gasp for fresh air." This statement, of course, tells us more about Mr. Douglas than about the book, which he did not name. There seemed, however, some chance that he might repeat his *Well of Loneliness* performance. But the authorities refused to be drawn, and the only result was that next day thousands of orders for *The Other Half* by John Worby could not be met from stock.

The book deals with the underworld created by modern economic conditions on both sides of the

"To Beg I Am Ashamed"

Atlantic. The life of the hobo and the tramp is realistically, and I believe truthfully, depicted. Lady Richmond addressed a more restrained protest about the sexual incidents in the book to the *Spectator*. Apparently the well-to-do mind can support with fortitude the sufferings of the down-and-out, but not the idea that he has any sex life.

A more recent episode of a similar character did not end so happily. The end of March 1938 promised to be dull for the popular press. There was a natural reaction in political news after the intense excitement caused by Hitler's occupation of Austria. The usually fruitful fields of crime and sport were for the moment barren of "sensations." And so on Tuesday the 29th, the *Daily Mail* fell back on the none too original expedient of finding "a disgraceful book." A special placard announced the discovery, and readers of the paper were presented with a denunciation of an autobiography entitled *To Beg I Am Ashamed*, which was about to be published by Messrs. George Routledge & Sons. The editor, who had not read the book but who had made "an examination of its contents," pleaded that it should never be published. The publishers made a dignified and reasoned protest in the correspondence columns of the *New Statesman and Nation* on the following Saturday:

SIR,
   On March 24th copies of a book entitled *To Beg I Am Ashamed* by Sheila Cousins were sent by us for review to the press. In the printed note accompanying each review

Above All Liberties

copy, the date of publication of the book was clearly stated —April 4th. It has for long been established as between publishers and press that books sent for review shall not be "noticed" in the press before the stated date of publication—a practice that has been developed to ensure fair treatment and equal opportunity to every newspaper. A copy of *To Beg I Am Ashamed* was sent with the date of publication marked in the usual way to the Editor of the *Daily Mail*; yet six days before publication the *Daily Mail* broke through the custom and courtesy of the publishing trade, and launched a violent attack on the book.

We are not concerned at the moment with either the moral attitude or the literary judgment of the *Daily Mail*, but we do wish to call attention to this breach of custom, courtesy and fair dealing by the *Daily Mail's* Editor.

A serious position will arise for press and publishers if, following the precedent of the *Daily Mail*, newspaper editors consider themselves at liberty, if they think fit, to override the established custom and attack, praise, or otherwise publicise books sent to them for review, before the date of publication of these books. It will probably not be difficult for a newspaper editor to convince himself that there is some peculiar pretext of urgency to justify him in breaking in future a long-established custom of fair dealing. We hope, however, that in calling attention to this action of the *Daily Mail*, and pointing to its dangers, we may help to prevent the chaos which might result from repetitions of such action.

GEORGE ROUTLEDGE AND SONS, LTD.

Broadway House,
   68–74, Carter Lane, E.C.4.

In the meantime, however, things had been moving. The *Daily Mirror* had taken up the cry on the Thurs-

"To Beg I Am Ashamed"

day. A placard read "A Vile Book." A full-page article denounced the book as "the vilest that has ever left the modern printing press," quoted passages and assured the reader (who must have found the excerpts rather dull) that there was more that "could appear in no newspaper." The Public Morality Council had sent a copy to the Home Secretary; and the *Daily Mail's* appeal had been wholeheartedly endorsed on the Friday by the *Spectator*.[1] The same day the publishers were visited by the police and decided to withhold the book for reasons which they explained in a letter published in the *New Statesman and Nation* and in *Time and Tide* the following week. Both these periodicals also contained articles sympathetic to the publishers. The letter read as follows:

SIR,

We regret that by withholding publication of *To Beg I Am Ashamed*, by Sheila Cousins, we may seem to many of your readers and to other members of the public to have refused to fight for a principle worth fighting for. May we therefore take this opportunity of placing before your readers the exact position in which we found ourselves on Saturday morning last, April 2nd?

On the evening of Friday, April 1st, we were visited by an inspector and a sergeant of the City Police for the second time that day, and they, acting on instructions from a high official authority, informed us that unless *To Beg I*

[1] This weekly used its review columns a year or two before to invite prosecution (which turned out to be successful) of a rubbishy transatlantic importation called *Indiscreet Confessions of a Nice Girl*.

Above All Liberties

Am Ashamed was withheld from publication "serious consequences might follow." We had before us also the views of our legal advisers, who stated that there was nothing indecent in the book and nothing that contravened the law; but our legal advisers could not maintain, in view of previous cases of the kind, that should we proceed with publication and be prosecuted, their view of the book would be upheld in the magistrate's court in the City of London where the case would be tried.

We were also aware that a certain section of the press, by a gross breach of privilege as between publishers and press, had given to this book, before publication, a notoriety that it never deserved, and had attracted to it a public for which it was never intended; and this factor was bound to weigh heavily with us in coming to our final decision as to whether to proceed with publication or withhold from publication.

It seemed to us, therefore, that we had been driven into a hopeless position; on the one hand should we proceed with publication, we should indeed be fighting for a principle worth fighting for, but should be supplying a public, manufactured by a section of the press, with a book never intended for it. On the other hand should we withhold publication, we should deprive that public of the book, but be refusing the opportunity to fight for a principle which we hold dear.

We decided to withhold the book.

We still maintain, as we have always maintained, and a large number of public men and women and literary critics who have read the book, as well as our legal advisers concur in our opinion, that there is nothing salacious or indecent in the book. It is a genuine and authentic record written, in our opinion with dignity and reticence, untainted by that objectionable mixture of suggestiveness

"To Beg I Am Ashamed"

and sentimentality that might so easily have characterised a work of this kind. Essentially decent itself, it had, however, after a week of publicising by a section of the press become something of a quite different character. And that, we think, is perhaps the most grave result of what has happened in the press during the last week. We hope that the precedent of the *Daily Mail* and the *Daily Mirror* will not be followed. If it is, there is an end to all free expression of thought.

GEORGE ROUTLEDGE AND SONS, LTD.

Broadway House,
   68–74 Carter Lane, E.C.4.

The police court proceedings which the publishers might have had to face bear a very close resemblance to a witchcraft trial. Everyone in the Court knows what "obscenity" is, everybody is capable of smelling it out, but nobody can define it. I have seen a Crown advocate whose whole appearance and demeanour was redolent of the bar parlour and the smoking-room leer up at a distinguished witness and say: "You know what I mean by 'dirty,' don't you?" The police court might be avoided by a defendant who had the courage to follow Bradlaugh's example. He obtained a *certiorari* transferring *The Fruits of Philosophy* case to the High Court on the ground that the object of the pamphlet was (in the words of Lord Chief Justice Cockburn) "the legitimate one of promoting knowledge on a matter of human interest." Surely prostitution comes within that category?

The appearance and get-up of *To Beg I Am Ashamed*

Above All Liberties

was discreet and in good taste except perhaps for a removable band which proclaimed it "an authentic autobiography of a London prostitute." This band might well have made the book a popular item in the windows of shops which specialise in near-pornography and, worse still, are only too pleased to sell reputable books as pornography. These shops present a most difficult facet of the problem of administering the law of "obscene libel" to the authorities. A book which may be quite legitimately sold to the public by a respectable bookseller from an average stock may contribute to something approaching a public nuisance when displayed in a "rubber shop" window.

What of the book itself? The author's name is Sheila Cousins. It is a surprising fact that of its two hundred and eighty-three pages less than seventy are occupied with the subject of prostitution. The emphasis that has been thrown on this relatively small part of the autobiography is typical of English psychology. Every day during the rush hours English men and women are herded into already overcrowded tube carriages by bawling porters who only require to be provided with goads to make the likeness to a cattle train complete. The only time that any serious consideration has been given by the general public to these undignified scenes was when somebody suggested that the congestion was capable of being exploited for sexual amusement. When the popular

"To Beg I Am Ashamed"

press were looking for something to discredit the French stay-in strikes in 1937 they backed a sure winner by informing their readers that the strikes "led to immorality."

The rest of the book describes the author's childhood, her employment as a canvasser and in offices, her married life and her life in Malaya. True to form she was related to a clergyman of the Established religion. Her family were of the undeserving middle class who do not trouble about public school education, who spend money rather than save it, and who are more emotional than intellectual. In Sheila Cousin's case these shortcomings resulted in her being sent to an industrial school. Although the author largely attributes her subsequent career to her mother's example, it was this police court sentence, I think, that determined it by giving her an inferiority complex which always expected and incited the depravity rather than the nobility in men.

What provoked the attack on the book? There is nothing in it that could not be paralleled in some modern novel or other. It is devoid of physiological details. Certainly it is in "bad taste" in that the milder vocabulary of the streets is frequently employed. But this, I think, has literary justification. The author's mother's denunciation of the Chairman of the Bench who sent her away as "a grouse-shooting old bastard" is undoubtedly an adequate, if colloquial, description of more than one such exalted personage. The writer

Above All Liberties

is also impolite about the physical and sartorial deficiencies of social workers *et hoc genus omne*. She has no use for Christians who would save her by putting a Bible into one hand and a scrubbing brush into the other. But I believe that the real sin of the book in the eyes of its execrators is that, like *Bessie Cotter*, it throws the hard light of realism on a calling that the orthodox prefer either to be made the subject of music-hall jokes or to be enveloped in a melodramatic haze of horror. The truth is that the London streets offer an untrained girl with certain physiological and psychological aptitudes a livelihood no less secure, no more dangerous, less dreary and better paid and with no worse prospects than that provided by respectable employment. The book brings out this fact clearly. It is a deplorable fact. But the cure is not to ban the book but to improve social conditions so that it is no longer true.

On the other hand, the author surrounds her calling with none of the glamour with which it is presented on the vaudeville stage. The emotional starvation which often finds relief in relations with a bully, the squalor, the close association with crime, are all clearly demonstrated. The humiliation of police persecution (generally intensified toward the end of the month when the constables must make up their quota of arrests) is portrayed with bitter and convincing realism. Some of the author's comments on her trade are illuminating:

"To Beg I Am Ashamed"

I regret that I was born and came on the streets in the age when I did. There is a tag, I believe, about the prostitute defending the virtue of the middle-class man's sister. That was true once, thirty years ago, and then were the high days of prostitution. The street-walker's client was the normal man who had yet to persuade his friend's sister that his intentions were honourable. To-day, with honourable intentions at a discount everywhere, my pick-ups are the rejects, the neurotics, the cast-outs who, for all the general promiscuity, have been unable to find a real woman for themselves.

She gives some detail of the curious and varied wants (not all physical) of these unhappy creatures. She has no emotional sympathy with them, but seems to have some understanding that they are the inevitable products of our system of sexual morals rather than the carriers of an extra dose of original sin. Like all valid studies of the subject, her book shows prostitution to be a measure of the inadequacy of the prevailing marriage law and sexual custom.

In their Annual Report, the Public Morality Council took considerable unction to themselves for the part they had played in this banning. It would be interesting to learn what lesson they and other "moralists" concerned expected the unfortunate author to draw from their victory. That she should devote herself more assiduously to her regular profession in future? It is to be hoped that she was not too deeply discouraged. She wrote a book that any intelligent man or woman could read with interest. Her mistake

Above All Liberties

was to try to publish it in a country where literary expression is so much under the censorship of the priest and the prig. In America, I believe, she would have been allowed to have her say with impunity.

CHAPTER VIII

CONTRAST WITH U.S.A.

THE English law of "obscene libel" obtains in substance throughout the English-speaking parts of the British Empire although there are local variations. Its effects in the Dominions have been much the same as in the home country, and there has been more than one instance of its unjust operation. In Australia a book called *The Answer* by W. J. Chidley was condemned in 1915. Chidley was a high-minded, if eccentric, philosopher, who walked about Sydney almost nude preaching a return to nature in diet, clothing and conduct. His book consists of a history of philosophy and answers the questions raised thereby with a serious, if somewhat fantastic, treatment of the technique of sexual congress in human beings. The magistrate who presided at the trial said that no philosophical work would be read by the public if it did not contain indecencies. Ellis treats Chidley seriously from the technical angle in the *Studies*, and more generally in *The Dance of Life*.

The United States of America retained the English common law, but judicial and legislative developments so far as literary "obscenity" is concerned have differed from those in England while of recent years there has been a marked contrast of very considerable interest.

Above All Liberties

For nearly four centuries after Columbus the new world knew nothing of literary "obscenity" laws. The import of foreign pornography was forbidden but this was an anti-foreign rather than a Puritan provision. Literary freedom was only curtailed in respect of women and negroes. In some states it was a crime to offer a Bible to a negro. But the white man was not considered to require the protective attention of the law in the selection of his reading.

During the nineteenth century, however, amid all the novelty and variety of the new world, there sprang up a prudery which sometimes outdid in extravagance the Victorianism of the old world. It is not uncommon for ideas to assume fantastic shapes in the exuberant transatlantic atmosphere. In certain circles "leg" became a forbidden word. It was found indelicate to mention the tail, the hip, or the thigh of an animal. A preacher in Georgia bowdlerised the Bible, reading "stomach" for "belly" and "a certain fowl" for "cock." It was in the States that the supporting members of the piano had to be draped. Captain Marryat tells us that at a ladies' seminary which he visited each piano leg was clothed in "modest little trousers, with frills at the bottom of them." He also relates that when he visited the Governor of Massachusetts, he saw in his house an Apollo Belvedere which was usually covered up "in compliance with general opinion." In 1840 there was much concern at

Contrast With U.S.A.

the display of Hirma Powers' statue, "The Greek Slave," at Cincinnati.

Charles Knowlton was fined in one Massachusetts town and imprisoned in another for publishing his *Fruits of Philosophy* in 1832. This pamphlet was subsequently made famous the world over by the Bradlaugh-Besant trial. About 1870 the legal situation as regards literary decency underwent a great change. The notorious Anthony Comstock rose to power. Federal and State legislation became the order of the day. Typical of this period was the fate of a charming and delicately written book of sex instruction for adolescent boys and girls entitled *Almost Fourteen* (1892) and of its author, M. A. Warren. The book was condemned as "obscene" in 1897 and the author forced to resign his appointment as a headmaster.

The mantle of the great Comstock fell on John S. Sumner. This Elisha does his best to follow in the steps of his Elijah, but he lacks Comstock's perverted genius, his cruelty, and his vindictiveness. Nevertheless, Sumner had Guerney, the translator of Gorky and Merejkowski, arrested on a charge of criminal libel for guying him in a cartoon. Ever since he succeeded Comstock as Secretary of the New York Society for the Suppression of Vice he has shown scant respect for art or letters. In 1923 he secured the withdrawal from publication of Schnitzler's *Casanova's Homecoming* by a prosecution which never came to trial. Seven years after the book was reprinted and

Above All Liberties

Sumner's renewed attack failed in the Courts. He was scarcely more successful against the same author's *Reigen*. In 1929 he secured a conviction, but very soon afterwards the book was reprinted with impunity. Against Donald Henderson Clarke's *Female* he launched two simultaneous prosecutions. One was successful, the other not; but the conviction was upheld on appeal. In 1927 he unsuccessfully prosecuted a translation of Flaubert's *Tentation de Saint-Antoine*; and a similar attack on André Gide's *Si le Grain ne Meurt* ended with the book's exoneration.

An amazing wave of censorship swept over Boston in the latter part of 1929, and a holocaust was made of over threescore books. The condemnations included the following list:

> *The Wayward Man* by St. John Ervine.
> *What I Believe* by Bertrand Russell.
> *Oil* by Upton Sinclair.
> *From Man to Man* by Olive Schreiner.
> *Power* by Leon Feuchtwanger.
> *Twilight* by Count Keyserling.
> *The World of William Clissold* by H. G. Wells.
> *The Hard-Boiled Virgin* by Frances Newman.
> *Elmer Gantry* by Sinclair Lewis.
> *Doomsday* by Warwick Deeping.
> *The Sun Also Rises* by Ernest Hemingway.

The following year the Massachusetts Supreme Court upheld the conviction of Donald S. Friede for selling

Contrast With U.S.A.

Theodore Dreiser's *An American Tragedy*. (The same author's *The Genius* had been suppressed in 1916.) At the same time the Court upheld the conviction of a reputable Boston bookseller who had been trapped into selling a copy of D. H. Lawrence's *Lady Chatterley's Lover* to an *agent provocateur* employed by the New England Watch and Ward Society. The method of obtaining commission of the crime was adversely commented on by the Court, the prosecuting counsel, and the Boston press. Mr. Sumner, who claimed to have instigated the whole thing, justified the use of the *agent provocateur* on the ground that he had information that the bookseller was supplying copies of *Lady Chatterley* to Harvard professors!

The Boston convictions focussed public attention on the Massachusetts obscenity law. The relevant statute forbade the public sale of any book "*containing* obscene indecent language." Enlightened opinion forced a change to the words "a book which *is* obscene, indecent." This presumably means that the book must be considered in its entirety.

Some reform has also been obtained in relation to the powers of the Customs in relation to "obscenity." Prior to 1930 they were able to behave in a very arbitrary manner. Anything which the officials judged "obscene" could be confiscated without trial. A trial was only necessary if an aggrieved person was sufficiently wealthy and persistent to bring the case into Court himself. This is still substantially the position

Above All Liberties

in England. The American officials used their power to exclude such authors as Aristophanes, Defoe, Petronius, Rabelais, Boccaccio, Balzac, Rousseau, Casanova and Voltaire in a most wholesale fashion. At the same time scientific works of recognised European reputation were seized. At last a young Baltimore attorney carried a case of seizure of *Daphnis and Chloë* by Longus and other books into Court. He won a brilliant victory. Further indefensible seizures caused public agitation and finally the law was amended by the Tariff Act of 1930. In the first place, if seizure was contested, the Government and not the aggrieved person had to press proceedings in the Courts. Secondly, the Secretary of the Treasury was given discretion to admit classics or books of recognised literary or scientific merit, even if obscene. As a result the Customs lifted the ban on Voltaire, Rabelais, Boccaccio and many other authors without judicial compulsion. Shortly afterwards the consignee of one hundred and twenty seized copies of Dr. Johannes Rutgers' *The Sexual Life in Its Biological Significance* forced the issue to litigation and won a favourable verdict from the jury. In spite of improvements, however, the American Customs frequently perpetrate amazing follies. In 1933 they seized reproductions of a copy of the famous frescoes in the Sistine Chapel made before Daniele da Volterra had, at the command of Pope Paul IV, painted loin cloths on Michelangelo's heroic figures. Work by Eric Gill

Contrast With U.S.A.

has also been stopped, as also a copy of George Ryley Scott's *Encyclopaedia of Sex* (1939).

Generally speaking, the tide may be said to have turned against Comstockery when Judge Woolsey exonerated James Joyce's *Ulysses* in 1933. This was the first of a series of enlightened decisions which have secured for the United States of America a measure of literary freedom which compares favourably with that enjoyed by this country, as we have already seen exemplified in more than one instance. No one has contributed more to this state of affairs than Mr. Morris Ernst, a lawyer who has fought case after case in the Courts with ability, courage and success. Mr. Sumner has sustained a corresponding series of humiliating defeats. The most recent of these was the failure of the prosecution of the Vanguard Press before the New York City Magistrate's Court on February 11, 1937, for publishing *The World I Never Made*, a novel by James T. Farrell. The magistrate (Hon. Henry M. Curran) refused to commit the case for trial in a decision full of breezy common sense which contrasts in a refreshing way with the humbugging treatment meted out to *To Beg I Am Ashamed*. The two books appear to be somewhat alike in the nature of their offence to censorial susceptibility. After some introductory remarks Mr. Curran proceeded:

There are coarse words in the book. There are old Saxon words, as they call them in some cases. I suspect that

Above All Liberties

after all they are known to practically everybody. A good many of them are there—too many, I think. There are coarse episodes as well, and there are erotic episodes. But neither the words nor the episodes that may be lewd or lustful or lecherous or libidinous or lascivious or licentious —all the adjectives seem to begin with "l"—are sufficient by themselves to condemn the book. The whole book must be considered. The question is, do these words and episodes change this book from a portrayal of life, or however else it may be described, as a whole, into an obscene print? It seems to me, to begin with, that if we are going to hang this book because of words and episodes that are detached from the whole book, that are picked out and isolated by themselves, disregarding the interest and disregarding the old Latin motto that I have not seen for so many years, *noscitur a sociis*, we have got to hang a good many other writings. I think we have got to begin with Homer and his *Odyssey*. We have got to condemn parts of the Bible, a good deal of Chaucer and certainly some of Shakespeare, quite a little of Fielding. . . .

There are also some painters some people object to. There is Rubens, in his rather gross painting of flesh. I, untutored, do think that I can go by Rubens pretty easily in our uptown art gallery and get along to Rembrandt. A question of taste perhaps. . . . We must not place ourselves in a position where we "cannot see the forest for the trees," where we cannot see the picture for the flyspecks. . . . Then, too, there are constant changes in our talk and in what is talked about. There are changes in the fashion of it from decade to decade and from century to century, and they are changes not only in the words themselves but in the freedom or restriction with which some of the words are ordinarily used. Even in ordinary conversation there is change. The contrast between Elizabethan

Contrast With U.S.A.

times in this respect is so sharp that we need only mention it. . . .

Then consider the young ladies in their bathing suits nowadays, how they toil not neither do they spin, but the Gibson girl in all her glory was not arrayed like one of these. If one of those lovely creatures of the far away nineties had really appeared in one of the little forget-me-not suits of to-day, I fancy there would have been a commotion on the beach—and the rockers on the summer hotel piazza would have rocked hard and long. . . .

So is it a question of taste here or is it a question of obscenity? Are some of the words and some of the episodes incidental to what the author is trying to do or are they lugged in? They may even be lugged in, quite beyond the bounds of what you and I may like, and still they may not be there for an obscene purpose. Some of the episodes objected to in the book are just repellent, and so are some of the words. So are some aspects of life. . . .

The strange thing is that near the end of the book I encountered, for the first time and with dismay, one of my pet abominations, and that is the only time that it occurs in the whole book. There is just one word where the author gives you the first letter and the last letter and between the two is a dash. In the old days, the way they used to write damn was "d—n."

Now in some of the little fights that wind up in the magistrates' court, if one person calls another a bum—and that often happens—you might write it "b—m." Or occasionally one citizen addresses another citizen as "rat." That usually produces a high degree of physical activity. But we don't record the word "r—t."

Words ought to be printed in full or left out altogether. Spell them or leave them out. I don't know what this mangled word means and I'm sure I don't want to know.

Above All Liberties

Maybe Mr. Sumner was looking over the author's shoulder while he wrote that page. In any event it's an abomination, that sort of thing. It makes a printed page look like a rail fence.

To sum up somewhat, this book is a powerful picture of the life of its people in South Chicago twenty-five years ago. . . . It may be in some part autobiographical. At least the author saw, and saw with keen eyes. It is a kind of life that is not all pleasant. It is extremely unpleasant in places. I think that is why the author wanted to give us a picture of it. . . .

It is fair to say, too, that there are beautiful episodes in the story. . . . I liked especially the part where the little boy Danny reminds Santa Claus that he sent him a letter and he didn't get an answer to it and he wants to know if Santa Claus got that letter, and furthermore, if Santa Claus is going to come through with the presents requested in the letter. I know I wrote a letter like that once. So have we all.

I found myself possessed also of a wish from time to time to get a little money somehow to a wife named "Liz" to fix her teeth. I couldn't see any way of fixing her teeth—and they were very bad. If she were only in my magistrates' court I could have looked out for her.

No, I don't think the book is pornographic. I think it is photographic, and something more. Certainly this author has a passion to show us that kind of life as he lived it, and he has "given it to us good," as the expression goes. . . .

I do not think it is an obscene book, an obscene exploit. I do not believe that it offends the statute, and therefore the warrant is vacated and the defendant is discharged.

Commenting on the result, Mr. Farrell said: "There are few enough countries left where a writer

Contrast With U.S.A.

can strive to write seriously and frankly. I am glad that America still remains one of them." It would have been truer to say "is becoming one of them."

As a result of Anthony Comstock's activities, the United States of America has been much less free than Great Britain so far as birth control is concerned. But the long war against the Comstock Act of 1873 in its relation to contraceptive literature, begun by the courageous Margaret Sanger in the lifetime of its author, was brought within sight of a victorious conclusion in April 1938. In that month a decision of the United States Circuit Court of Appeals was given against the Government in *U.S. v. Certain Magazines (Marriage Hygiene)*.[1] The Court held that contraceptive literature could enter the U.S.A. under the Tariff Act without interference on the part of the Collector of Customs, provided the consignee, even though a layman, was a person qualified to receive it. The lawyers for the defence made the following statement:

> We have won a very important legal victory, and one that is likely to have a highly salutary effect on the treatment accorded by lower courts to contraceptive books and materials. Prior to this decision, it was the policy of the Government to stop all contraceptive literature at the customs regardless of the identity of the consignee. We now have an adjudication that such literature may freely enter, *provided* the consignee is a person qualified to

[1] See Mr. Norman E. Himes in the *Eugenics Review*, October 1938. Himes appears to publish his own monumental and scholarly work on birth control without legal molestation.

Above All Liberties

receive it. The qualifications of the consignee may be established by a mere affidavit, and the procedure is very simple.

In America the man in the street seems to be establishing his right to sexual knowledge on the same terms as other sorts of knowledge. The howl of disapproval with which the Church Assembly in England greeted a very modest quota of sex instruction contained in a book published by the Student Christian Movement in 1939 showed how difficult it is to convey such instruction to the general public. The book (*Education for Christian Marriage*, edited by A. S. Nash) contains a chapter of practical instruction sandwiched between great doorsteps of moral exhortation and dogmatic exposition. The chapter contains just enough information (and no more) than is necessary to ensure that a newly married couple would not risk failure and humiliation in their first experiences of being alone and uncontrolled. Contrast this with *How to Achieve Sex Happiness in Marriage* published the same year by Henry and Freida Thornton in New York, a completely outspoken and straightforward account of all matters covering the sex side of married life. Yet twenty years ago such books as Dr. Robie's *Art of Love* were judged "obscene."

Any generalisation about the United States should be treated with caution. Differences in law and administration between states, conflict between state and federal law, and even disparity in attitude between

Contrast With U.S.A.

departments of the federal administration, all make for a variety and an uncertainty even greater than that attending the operation of the law of obscene libel in England. The New York Book of the Month Club bowdlerised the translation of Remarque's *Im Westen nichts Neues* (1929), and the publishers instigated the New York Customs to exclude the integral English edition. The Roman Catholic Church constantly exploits to the best of her ability the chaotic state of affairs in the interests of obscurantism. On the West Coast the law has been perverted to secure the banning of John Steinbeck's *Grapes of Wrath* (1939) in the interests of employers in California's fruit and vegetable industry. The book, a sort of modern *Uncle Tom's Cabin*, exposes the virtual enslavement of the workers.

The motive was similar to that which, some years earlier, caused the arrest of Upton Sinclair for selling *Oil*. The Library Committee of East St. Louis, a suburb of Chicago, passed a resolution to burn the five copies of this book in their custody. The protests of the National Council on Freedom from Censorship were, however, so vigorous that the resolution was rescinded, and the only result was an increased demand for the book from borrowers. The efforts of enlightened professors to find out what students really think about sex matters by means of questionnaires have been suppressed by University authorities.

Lest this chapter should conclude on too optimistic

Above All Liberties

a note, I will end it with some extracts from a lively report on actual conditions sent me by a correspondent:

The big thing is the Postal Department. They decide what can and cannot be advertised by mail—which includes newspaper and magazine advertising, since these have mailing permits for subscriptions, and their rule is that anything with "sex" in the title is obscene, and lots of other things too. . . . The Post Office can put a mail-order out of business by refusing to accept its circular mail, and when that doesn't work it prosecutes. . . . The most important case recently was that of the Falstaff Press, a rather unsavoury organisation that sent out hundreds of thousands of lurid circulars to sell *expurgated* editions of standard German, French and Italian works of sexual science, such as those of Moll, Bloch, Tarnowski, Mantegazza, etc. Since the stuff was not obscene except to the old attitude that anything on sex is indefensible (which has been rather hard to maintain of recent years in the light of civilised decisions by the Justices Maud and others) some other method of "getting" the Falstaff Press was indicated, and was found. . . . The Post Office rushed a precedent through in the case of a street peddler who pretended to be selling obscene cartoon booklets in the streets . . . a precedent stating that since he offered merchandise purporting to be obscene and which actually were not obscene, he was guilty of fraud. . . . On these grounds the Falstaff circulars were held to imply that the books advertised were obscene (that is, pertained to sex) and that the books actually were not (as, of course, they weren't), and so Falstaff stood convicted of fraud, and was held in exorbitant bail and the hearing continually postponed until the lack of capital put the business on the rocks. The case was appealed—after a

Contrast With U.S.A.

new trial had been granted, and this time the books were held by an old-time judge to be obscene—and the decision upheld. An immense fine was collected (to take away all the "ill-gotten" profits . . . i.e. to keep Falstaff from building up so big a business again) and a suspended sentence given, although jail sentences of two and three years have been handed out since 1930 in sex book cases. The suppression of pornography is very lackadaisical. The Post Office answers all shady advertisements of this type—e.g. for nude "art" photographers, "spicy" correspondence clubs. . . . The answers are, of course, sent from fake names, and the pounce is not made at once, every possible contact being sought. Then when really obscene merchandise is offered, they grab off the seller, sweat him till he squeals on his source of supply, and so on down the line till they have a bunch of defendants. Often when they have done their work too well, "spicy" magazines are out of business, and scape-goats are few; the postal inspectors will bait some poor bookseller with repeated orders for legitimate books (occasionally thousands of dollars have been spent this way over a period of two or three years, just to get one suspected dealer) and then ring in a fishy order for "Fanny Hill" or "Grushenka" or "Josephine Mutzenbacher" and so on. Then the carefully manufactured felon is thrown into jail. . . . Another aspect of the racket is the custon department's part. The customs inspectors keep a black list, and add to it all the time. Erotic books are of course on it, and many scientific sex books—particularly those with pictures, which even a customs inspector can be expected to understand. . . . Even in luggage much is seized, as the customs inspectors are uneducated persons as a usual thing, who get their jobs through political pull, and they have the usual resentment of the uneducated for culture. I have seen a pair of thick-

Above All Liberties

necked boors in brass buttons descend on some professional looking individual and tear hell out of a trunk full of books, crumpling pages, smearing covers, comparing titles with a grimy list, and dragging open a heavy quarto on Rome or the Renaissance with a snap that cracks the binding, pointing to a nude or to the penis of a horse on a Grecian urn, and snorting "Science, huh?" with the most withering of scorn. . . .

CHAPTER IX

OUTRAGE AUX MŒURS

BEFORE the present war many an English-speaking man saw France through rosy spectacles. To him it was a land singularly free from those restrictions with regard to alcoholic refreshment, the theatre, and literature which he supports with more or less bad grace at home. To cross the Channel or the Atlantic was to leave the reign of Mrs. Grundy behind and to enter a realm where the ideal of moral liberty was carried to its logical conclusions without compromise and without hypocrisy. He found this contrast particularly marked in regard to the highly controversial questions of decency and obscenity in literature. Certain books by reputable authors suppressed in England or America found a refuge in Parisian bookshops where they appeared cheek by jowl with a quantity of ephemeral pornography that, whatever its merits or demerits, relied for its market chiefly on the British and American tourist traffic.

Let us examine the facts behind this very superficial picture of paradisal literary freedom. We must base our inquiry on the state of affairs which existed in 1939. What changes the war may bring about it is impossible to predict, and no reliable information is available as to changes that may have already taken place.

Above All Liberties

The French equivalent to our "obscene libel" is the "*outrage aux bonnes mœurs.*" This offence must be distinguished from *outrages publics à la pudeur* (Art. 330 of the *Code Pénal*) which concerns the exhibition of indecent actions; and also from *attentat aux mœurs* which is equivalent to our rape and indecent assault.

Current law relating to *l'outrage aux bonnes mœurs* is contained in Art. 28 of the *Loi du 29 Juillet* 1881, and in the *Loi Spéciale du 2 Août* 1882 as amended by the *Loi du Mars* 1898 and the *Loi du Avril* 1908.

The Law of 1881 ("*sur la liberté de la presse*") was a huge codification of press law repealing previous legislation and covering every medium of publication. It also covered oral expression. Article 28 dealt with the offence of "*l'outrage aux bonnes mœurs.*" Penalties were a month to two years' imprisonment and fines of 16 to 2,000 francs. Perpetual loss of electoral rights followed conviction *ipso facto*. Prosecution had to take place within a year of publication or introduction into French territory. A distinction was made between drawings, prints, engravings and paintings, on the one hand, and all other mediums of publication on the other. Offenders by means of the latter were triable by jury at the Cour d'Assises and enjoyed certain privileges allowed to press offences; offenders by means of the former were triable at Police Correctionelle (paid magistrates sitting without a jury) and were treated as common law criminals.

Outrage Aux Mœurs

This law was immediately taken advantage of by publishers of more or less gross pamphlets and periodicals which, being unillustrated, could only be dealt with by rather slow and clumsy arraignment before a jury. Something like a public nuisance was met by the law of 1882 which modified Article 28 of the law of 1881. All mediums of publication other than books and the spoken word (e.g. newspapers, periodicals, pamphlets and all sorts of pictures) were made triable by the Police Correctionelle. The offence was extended to cover the sale, offering for sale, or advertisement of books already condemned. Penalties were a month to two years' imprisonment, and a fine of 100 to 5,000 francs. If the offence was against minors the penalties could be doubled. Five years' loss of electoral rights followed a sentence of imprisonment exceeding six days. Any condemned matter could be seized or destroyed.

The law of 1898 brought within the scope of the law of 1882 book illustrations, obscene objects and correspondence in journals. Fines were raised and songs and public utterances (as distinct from speeches), which previously could only be dealt with by the Cour d'Assises under the law of 1881, were brought within the jurisdiction of the Police Correctionelle under the law of 1882. This amendment was made on the initiative of Senator Réné Bérenger, whose zeal in these matters earned him the sobriquet of Bérenger-la-Pudeur. The law of 1908 brought non-public commerce, drawings and writings other than books within the scope of the law of 1882.

This amendment was initiated in the Senate and, as first passed in that Chamber, was a much more severe affair. Among other provisions, the manufacture and keeping of obscene objects was made criminal, and newspaper advertisements and correspondence having obscene purposes were declared contrary to *bonnes mœurs*. The Chamber of Deputies, however, refused to follow *les pères conscrits* so far. Both the provisions quoted evoked spirited protests, and Deputies of all parties rallied to the defence of the inviolable and sacred rights of the citizen. The Government had to content itself with the comparatively small amendment quoted which passed the Senate in spite of vociferous protests against its mildness on the part of Senator Bérenger, whose crusading zeal only increased with age.

To complete the picture of current French law affecting the expression of sexual ideas, a provision contained in the "Law Repressing the Provocation of Abortion and the Propaganda of Contraception," passed in 1920, must be mentioned. The spreading of contraceptive knowledge by any means is forbidden under severe penalties. This law, of course, resulted in the break-up of the Malthusian League in France. Even before the passing of the law, in 1909, the Tribunal Correctionelle de Rouen condemned as an *outrage aux mœurs* the distribution of an announcement of

Outrage Aux Mœurs

a Neo-Malthusian Conference. In the same spirit the Tribunal Civil de Lille condemned a similar announcement as a *prospectus d'une ligue immorale et anti-sociale*. The exponents of what the profane term *le lapinisme* are therefore well armed in law. A Belgian prosecution of Knowlton's famous *Fruits of Philosophy* in 1900 was, we may note, happily unsuccessful.

It will be seen that French law with regard to the expression of sexual ideas is quite as severe as the English common law taken into conjunction with Lord Campbell's Act; and furthermore the spoken word is subject to the same restriction as the written word.

But what precisely constitutes an *outrage aux bonnes mœurs*? When Sir Archibald Bodkin boasted before the International Conference for the Suppression of Obscene Publications at Geneva in 1923 that there was no statutory definition of obscenity in English law, the French delegates might with equal satisfaction have declared that a definition of *outrage aux bonnes mœurs* was equally far to seek. The best that English law can do in the way of a definition of obscenity is an *obiter dictum* of Lord Chief Justice Cockburn in *R.* v. *Hicklin* which, as we have seen, has crept into the text-books as established law. It is so wide and loose that almost any writing with a sexual content which excites the animosity of a knave or upsets the susceptibilities of a fool can be brought within its bounds. France is little better. There is no

Above All Liberties

definition of *outrage aux bonnes mœurs* in any of the laws quoted nor in any other enactment of the French legislature. '*Le legislateur a été impuissant a donner une définition de l'outrage aux bonnes mœurs,*" says M. Albert Eyqueum of the Académie des Sciences Morales et Politiques in his celebrated *De la Répression des outrages à la morale publique ou de la Pornographie* (Paris, 1905). When the Law of 1882 was being debated it was reported that a Commission of the Chamber of Deputies had vainly attempted a definition: all that could be done was to lay down the means by which the offence could be committed (*Journal Officiel* of June 8th). A definition can therefore only be sought in the pronouncements of the Courts, and in the works of those learned writers on jurisprudence who count so much more in French than in English practice.

Only M. le Conseiller Mouton in his *Lois pénales de la France* is sure of his ground:

> *La morale publique n'est pas telle loi, telle religion, tel precepte, telle institution, telle erreur, c'est la Morale même, cele que rien ne peut attendre, que rien ne peut obscurcir, qui est immuable, incorruptible, éternelle, absolue comme la Vérité dont elle n'est qu'une face.*

But his certitude is not of a kind easily communicated to minds less theological than his own. Senator Bérenger himself was alone more confident.

> *On croit nous embarrasser en nous demandant des définitions. L'abbé Sertillanges a dit excellemment: est obscène tout*

Outrage Aux Mœurs

e qui trouble la chair. J'a'outerai est immoral tout ce qui peut corrompre l'enfant.

The esteemed M. Eyqueum is only helpful in a negative way. Obscenity, he holds, is essentially mercenary and base. Works of art and literature cannot be considered obscene even if unsuitable for minors. A *Traité de la Presse* by M. le Poiteau supports this view:

> *Il faut toujours considérer le but poursuivi par l'auteur. Si celui-ci s'est proposé de faire une œuvre serieuse, une œuvre qui soit vraiment artistique ou littéraire, peu importent certain détails que le sujet même a pu rendre necessaires.*

M. Barbier in his *Code expliqué de la Presse* maintains that the Law of 1882 is concerned with obscenity properly so called which according to him is *"Le licencieux qui s'étale brutalement, qui ne se dissimule pas sous les voiles de l'art; le licencieux aggravé par la grossièreté de la forme."* He held that: *"La loi tolère la publication qui va jusqu'à la licence sans atteindre l'obscène."*

In 1900, however, the Tribunal de Limoges condemned certain reproductions of paintings by Boucher, Watteau and Lancret because *"l'intention évidente de l'auteur est d'exciter les passions sensuelles."* The defendant was also sentenced to three months' imprisonment for publishing a brochure which *"soit par des allusions et des descriptions dont la transparence ne peut tromper personne, définit l'acte charnel et les parties qui doivent demeurer cachées de l'homme et de la femme."*

Above All Liberties

The most authoritative judgment is that of the Court of Cassation in 1892 stating that a defendant "*faisait vendre, à bas prix, les détails les plus circonstanciés sur l'organisation du système génital avec des gravures le répresentant . . . que ce fait caractérise le délit d'outrages aux bonnes mœurs, etc.*"

The Courts have consistently refused to entertain ingenious attempts to circumvent the law. In 1908 the Tribunal de la Seine held that an advertisement of a brothel under the guise of a massage establishment was not illegal. But the judgment was reversed by the Cour d'Appel de Paris. The same attitude is illustrated by a very early case. In 1855 an ironmonger was charged before the 3rd Chambre Correctionelle de la Seine for selling "*des vases de nuit au fond desquels s'étalait, peint sur émail un grand œil ouvert accompagné de cette legende: 'Je te vois.'*" The complainant was a rival tradesman probably more jealous than virtuous. The defendant was sentenced to a month's imprisonment. The sentence was confirmed, on appeal, where the defendant's advocate made an energetic defence. What was culpable about either the eye or the lettering? "*De brandir son pot de chambre et de l'exposer à l'auditoire,*" he claimed that the resulting laughter came not only from the gentlemen present but also from the ladies (whose respectability was above question). His client had only made a joke—a Billingsgate joke, perhaps, but only a joke—and a joke was not an offence. Counsel for the prosecution

Outrage Aux Mœurs

was, however, adamant. He was not arraigning either the picture or the lettering, but their position. The Court would appreciate that. And the Court did.

The date of this last case makes it clear that the offence of literary or graphic indecency was not originated by the law of 1881. The historian might find its origin comprised in the famous ordinance of Charles IX:

Il est défendu de publier aucun écrit en rime ou en prose, sans la permission du seigneur Roy, sous peine d'être pendu ou étranglé.

But before the Revolution of 1789, however, the most cognate offence known to the law was writing against religion. As in England, the preoccupation of authority was with blasphemy and sedition. If indecency was condemned it was because it attacked the clergy or the King. It may be noted that the song held something like a privileged position, and was from the time of Villon the acknowledged vehicle for the sallies of Gallic wit against authority, sanctity, and propriety. The licence of the Revolutionary period produced a spate of pornography which reached its apogee in the erotic nightmares of de Sade and the counterblasts of Rétif de la Bretonne. These and similar works were consigned by the First Consul to the Enfer of the Bibliothèque Nationale which he modelled on a similar institution in the Vatican Library. The revolutionaries themselves had, how-

Above All Liberties

ever, attempted to deal with the problem. In 1791 a Law, opposed by Robespierre, was passed making criminal public assaults on the modesty of women by indecent action; the exposure for sale of obscene pictures, and the corruption of young persons. Under Napoleon, in 1810, writing and songs were brought under the purview of the law. With the Restoration a reign of prudery started in real earnest. In 1819 a Law assimilated the offences of *outrage aux bonnes mœurs* and *outrage à la morale publique et religieuse*.

An early victim of this state of the law was the song writer Béranger, whose liberal and Bonapartist tendencies were offensive to the Monarchy. He was twice imprisoned and between his trials an enactment of 1821, among other reactionary provisions, withdrew the trial of the offence from juries. Later the law was invoked against reprints of Voltaire's *Pucelle*, while decrees forbade works by Rousseau, and l'Abbé Prévost, as well as the *Decameron* and the *Heptameron*. During this period Louvet de Couvray's *Amours du Chevalier de Faublas* was condemned no less than four times. First published in 1786 and 1789, this picture of aristocratic manners before the Revolution provoked Carlyle to a typical outburst of condemnatory rhetoric. The works of another writer of the old régime, Crébillon *le fils*, were condemned in 1852. In his lifetime the author had been banished from Paris by the outraged virtue of Madame de Pompadour. During the first three-quarters of the nineteenth

Outrage Aux Mœurs

century, it is scarcely an exaggeration to say that the French law attempted to re-edit the literature of previous ages: Ronsard, Piron, Choderlos de Laclos, and Mirabeau are other names among the authors of works condemned for obscenity.

Eighteen hundred and twenty-five is the date of one of the very few prosecutions in France of a scientific work of non-fiction. In that year Antoine Jacques Duluare, a prolific archaeologist and historian whose works are remembered with respect to-day, published a new edition of his *Des Divinités Génératrices* which had issued from the press twenty years before. The book is a learned study of the phallic element in the religions of all ages. Duluare's trenchantly expressed Republican and anti-Catholic opinions had made him many enemies in the new régime who were only waiting for an opportunity to settle their scores with him. The book was seized and condemned.

Reaction was unabated during the Second Empire. In 1853 the brothers Goncourt were prosecuted over a magazine article. The motives of the attack were really political, but an acquittal was only obtained on the personal intervention of the Emperor, who wished to avoid being made to look a fool. Under Napoleon III, Béranger's Bonapartist admirations brought him into official favour, and he was accorded national honours. But contemporary writers who were experimenting with new methods and new subjects were less fortunate. In the year of Béranger's death (1857)

Above All Liberties

two masters of the French language, one of prose, the other of verse, occupied in their turn the dock of the 6th Chambre Correctionelle de la Seine.

In January there was the celebrated prosecution of Flaubert over *Madame Bovary*, whose publication in serial form had just been completed. Flaubert was acquitted. But his counsel put forward the plea, familiar in English courts of law, that in depicting "vice" his client had done no more than seek to promote "virtue." This plea assumes that it is the business of literature to support the morality of the day, rather than "to hold as 'twere the mirror up to nature" and to subject the prevailing *mores* to intelligent criticism. In pronouncing their judgment, the magistrates made the most of their opportunity by reading the immortal Flaubert a long lecture on the relation of art to morality with little lack of assurance and less of banality.

In the summer came the turn of Baudelaire's *Fleurs du Mal*. The appearance of the book had been greeted with a great deal of abuse in the press, and the first attack on a volume of verse since the case of Béranger followed. Baudelaire did all he could to defend himself. He even appealed to the influential Sainte-Beuve for help. But the great critic felt that his respectability had already been compromised by some praise of *Madame Bovary* he had published in the *Moniteur*, and he could offer nothing but good advice. The prosecution adopted the procedure (not unknown in

Outrage Aux Mœurs

English obscenity cases) by which passages are taken out of their context and considered in isolation. Baudelaire protested and claimed that his book should be considered as a whole. At the trial counsel for the prosecution roundly denounced everything about the book from its contents to its low price. Six poems now read the world over were condemned and the poet was fined. In spite of the courtesy of the magistrates (the decision referred to "the poet" and not "the accused"), Baudelaire was astounded and mortified. He could not be comforted even by Victor Hugo's commiseration and encouragement:

Vos "Fleurs du Mal" rayonnent et éblouissent comme les étoiles. Continuez je crie: Bravo! de toutes mes forces à votre vigoureux esprit.

Like many another author in a similar predicament he thought that he could have done better than his counsel. The plea of exposing "vice" in the interests of "virtue" had again been put forward. Baudelaire was confident that if he had conducted his own case, and had asserted the absolute independence of art *vis-à-vis* morality, he would have been acquitted. He was wise enough, however, not to put this opinion to the test on appeal, but resolved to write six new poems *"beaucoup plus beaux que ceux supprimés."* By 1861 he brought out a new edition to which he supplied not six but thirty-five new poems. He intended to preface this edition with a defence of his work, but

Above All Liberties

although he made three drafts the project was not carried out. The first version begins:

> Ce n'est pas pour mes femmes, mes filles ou mes sœurs que ce livre a été écrit; non plus que pour les femmes, les filles ou les sœurs de mon voisin. Je laisse cette fonction à ceux qui ont intérêt à confondre les bonnes actions avec le beau langage.

In 1866 the condemned poems along with fresh material appeared in a surreptitious publication under the title of *Les Épaves*.

Baudelaire's publisher in 1857 was Poulet-Malassis —known to his intimates as Coco-mal-perché. A rebus on his name decorated most of the books he issued, but it did not appear on the *Fleurs du Mal*. Poulet-Malassis had a flair for new and audacious talent, as well as a habit of reprinting provocative books that the authorities would rather have left forgotten. Against him the French law waged a war as bitter as that of Victorian prudery against Vizetelly, the publisher who popularised Zola in England. In *le grand procès de Lille* of 1868 sixty-three books, including works by Verlaine, Casanova, Mirabeau, and even Corneille were condemned.

The year 1857 saw the death of Eugène Sue, whose socialist and revolutionary views had been expressed in his *Mystères de Paris* and his *Mystères du Peuple*. He died while the latter work was being condemned on a large number of counts of which *outrage à la morale publique et religieuse et aux bonnes mœurs* was one.

Outrage Aux Mœurs

Political animus against extreme treatment of the problem of social justice continued into the early years of the Third Republic. In 1876 Jean Richepin was imprisoned on account of his *Chanson des Gueux*. The offence was *outrage à morale publique et religieuse et aux bonnes mœurs*; but the motive of the prosecution was largely fear of the political effects of Richepin's realistic pictures of the life of the "down and out." He published an eloquent protest in the *Tribune* on the morrow of the condemnation concluding thus:

J'ai peints les petits, les va-nu-pieds, les meurt-de-faim. J'ai tenté de montrer la boue dans laquelle la société les force à vivre; j'ai remué cette boue d'une main cynique, mais pitoyables. J'ai voulu y faire descendre un rayon de soleil; et on a trouvé cela malsain, immoral, monstrueux.

Je ne me suis pas érigé en docteur; je n'ai pas proposé de remède; mais j'ai dit simplement à la société:

"Voilà ce que tu fais des pauvres, respire leurs puanteurs, mets le doigt dans leurs plaies, vois grouiller leurs hontes, leurs vices, et frappe-toi la poitrine en songeant que tout cela se fait par te faute."

Et la société a fermé les yeux pour ne pas voir, s'est bouché le nez pour ne pas sentir, et, au lieu de frapper sur sa poitrine, a frappé sur la mienne.

En un mot, j'ai voulu faire chanter les Gueux, et les honnêtes gens viennent de me close la bouche brutalement, avec l'éternel cri de guerre des heureux: "*Les gueux n'ont pas le droit de parler. Silence aux pauvres!*"

"*Silence aux pauvres!*"—a prudent maxim, and the conception of obscenity one of the many aids to its enforcement.

Above All Liberties

The same year saw a remarkable Left-wing electoral victory, and an agitation for an amnesty in respect of political offences during the Commune of 1870 began. A short story called *Maudite* by Léon Cladel sought to aid this cause by depicting the sufferings of the wife of a deported Communarde forced into prostitution to support herself and her children. Both the author and the editor of the magazine in which it appeared were fined for *outrage aux bonnes mœurs*.

Unadulterated prudery was still, however, in the field. The year before a publisher was fined for reproducing the magnificent *fermiers généraux* edition de luxe of La Fontaine's *Contes*, in spite of the previous authorisation of the Minister of the Interior. The year before that the *Diaboliques* of Barbery d'Aurevilly was condemned to destruction although the author escaped conviction.

During this period a woman enters this long gallery of offenders. Mlle. Marie Amélie Chartroule (afterwards Mme. Quivogne) concealed her identity under the pseudonym: Marc de Montifaud. Before she was twenty she published her first book, *Les Courtesanes de l'antiquité, Marie-Magdeleine*, in which she elaborated a theory reminiscent of Marlowe's "Diabolical Opinion." As the book was published in Brussels, the authorities could do nothing except stop its entry into France. In 1876 she republished a book attributed to the seventeenth-century rake, Pierre Corneille-Blesse-

Outrage Aux Mœurs

bois, adding a preface which rivalled the original work in outspokenness. For this she was fined. The next year she was in Court over an original work entitled *Les Vestales de l'Église* dealing with the convents of the Middle Ages. This time she was sentenced to three months' imprisonment as well as a fine. At this period her offence was treated as a political one, but the only prison for women, the Saint-Lazarre, had no facilities for political detention. She refused to be mixed with its population of common criminals, and spent her three months in a nursing home under supervision. Another two of her books were consigned to the Enfer of the Bibliothèque Nationale, but have now been released.

In the following decade another girl, Mlle. Marguerite Eymery, published in Brussels under the pseudonym of Madame Rachilde a novel entitled *Monsieur Vénus*. According to her critics she practised the precept *lasciva est nobis pagina, vita proba*. Attacked by the Belgian Courts, she fled to France, where she continued an astonishing literary career.

One of the first victims of the new laws of 1881 and 1882 was Louis Desprez in respect of a naturalistic novel of peasant life entitled *Autour d'un Clocher*, written in collaboration with Henri Fèvre, a minor. Published in Belgium at the same time as Huysmans' *A Rebours* (1884) and other sensational books, this first essay of young blood was well on the way to passing unnoticed when it was seized in the book-

Above All Liberties

shops by the French authorities. Fèvre escaped prosecution because of his youth. Desprez before the Cour d'Assises de la Seine asserted the independence of art in an unqualified form and claimed that the only jury competent to try his work was one drawn from the masters of contemporary French literature: Victor Hugo, Edmond de Goncourt, Zola, Alphonse Daudet, etc. A jury of small tradesmen found him "Guilty," and he was sentenced to a month's imprisonment and a fine of one thousand francs. This was in effect a death sentence. Desprez suffered from hip disease which became complicated by tuberculosis. In vain Zola, Clemenceau, Daudet, Goncourt and others pleaded for a mitigation of the rigours of his prison. He died shortly after his release. The authorities were probably no more moved by this early death of a brilliant young writer than their English compeers cared about the similar end of honest old Vizetelly; but posterity will endorse the tersely expressed verdict of Zola: "*Ceux qui ont assassiné cet enfant sont des misérables.*"

Seven days after the trial of Desprez, Paul Bonnetain was indicted in respect of *Charlot s'amuse* (a novel dealing with masturbation) published the previous year, but the jury acquitted him.

The publisher of both the two last-mentioned books was the redoubtable Henri Kistemaeckers of Brussels, the publisher of Maupassant, Huysmans and other naturalist authors. Eighteen times prosecuted before Belgian juries, he was acquitted every time;

Outrage Aux Mœurs

prosecuted five times before magistrates without juries, he was thrice acquitted. Finally he took umbrage at a sharp sentence meted out after conviction in respect of advertisements in his journal *Le Flirt* and fled to France. The French authorities honourably refused to extradite him.

In 1889 Lucien Descaves published a novel called *Sous-offs*, exposing the petty tyranny and inefficiency of non-commissioned officers in the Army. Like Mr. Frank Griffin's book *I Joined the Army* (1937), it naturally did not find favour with the "brass-hats." General Boulanger supported a press agitation against it, and a prosecution for *outrages aux bonnes mœurs* and *injuries publique à l'armée* followed, but the jury acquitted on both counts.

During the eighties and nineties there were other prosecutions of contemporary novels, but they became less frequent and less important. In 1890 a question was raised in the Chamber of Deputies regarding a novel which although not legally attacked had been banned from the railway bookstalls. In 1892 an illustrated journal of the *Vie Parisienne* type was prosecuted before a Police Correctionelle under the Law of 1882 for publishing an extract from a novel which had not been attacked under the Law of 1881. In spite of the author's protests the prosecution was successful.

It is with periodicals (because they are amenable to the more summary law of 1882) rather than with

Above All Liberties

books, that the law has concerned itself in recent times. During the eighties and nineties a long struggle was maintained against the *Courrier Français,* a periodical revived by Jules Roques. Some of these prosecutions were not unconnected with "*La Ligue, contre l'Immoralité des Rues.*" Roques had given this body his ironical support, pretending to believe that it was protesting against the number of people found dead from hunger and cold in the streets during the terrible winter 1889–90. In 1896 a conviction was obtained, on the complaint of the indefatigable Senator Béranger, in respect of a poem by Hugues Delorme entitled *Les Aisselles.*

After the war a periodical called *Le Grand Guignol* made some violent attacks on M. Poincaré and M. Barthou. In August 1933 the editor was arrested on a number of criminal charges, all of which were dropped except that of *outrage aux bonnes mœurs.* Conviction on this charge produced a fine of one thousand francs and six months' imprisonment. In 1923 the editor of *Le Cupidon* was fined for quoting a page of Pietro Aretino and for publishing a short story called "*Le Robinet.*" The same year in the same court a woman was fined for quoting a passage from a novel (not prosecuted) when reviewing it. In 1926 a publisher was imprisoned for issuing a brochure containing articles and drawings from the *Cupidon.*

Of recent times there has been a tendency to hear

Outrage Aux Mœurs

these cases *à huis-clos*. This is comparable to that interpretation of the English law which allows reports of obscenity trials to be themselves prosecuted for obscenity, and makes intelligent criticism of the law extremely difficult.

Study of the operation of French law in regard to the expression of ideas on sexual subjects suggests that the French have little reason for throwing stones, as they sometimes do, at *la pudibonderie anglais*. The law itself is as severe as its English equivalent to which it bears some surprising resemblances. It is even wider in its scope since it covers the spoken as well as the written word. In both countries the conception on which the offence penalised rests is equally incapable of objective definition. Consequently the administration of the law is of necessity arbitrary in its nature and an expression of personal tastes and prejudices rather than a manifestation of the rule of law in the true sense of the term. In both countries those whose minds are obsessed with the conception of "obscenity" show the same indifference to the normal safeguards against infringement of individual liberty. They are equally reckless as regards injustice or even common humanity. In both countries they demand that art should be puerile, and literature conformable to the standards of the nursery. French literature, as well as English, has been subjected to the impertinent assaults of the "smut-hound." The masters of the past, together with the innovators of

Above All Liberties

the present, have been attacked. In neither country has repentance for past misdeeds been evidenced by amendment of the law. In France, nineteenth-century condemnations have quietly fallen into oblivion by the same process as now allows Englishmen to read Havelock Ellis and James Joyce. The soil of France is capable of breeding a vice crusader as fanatical as a Comstock or a Jix. The magistrates of France are capable of *sottises* quite comparable to the wisdom produced by English benches when they venture upon the unfamiliar fields of art and literature. There is the same susceptibility on the part of the authorities to press agitation. There is the same objection to sexual books priced so as to be within reach of the masses. Trade jealousy, commercial opportunism and even personal spite can masquerade under the cloak of outraged virtue as easily as in this country.

But when all is said and done there is a difference. Most strikingly, no scientific work has been condemned as obscene in France during modern times. The English have to their discredit the banning of Havelock Ellis's work, and the *Sexual Impulse* case in 1935 demonstrated that the spirit of the law has not markedly changed in the last forty years. No one thought of prosecuting the French edition of Havelock Ellis's great work. Again, no French student is debarred from consulting unbowdlerised translations into his own language of the Classics and foreign books. The reader of Lucian, Martial, Petronius *et*

Outrage Aux Mœurs

hoc genus omne in English is lucky if he knows where, and to what extent, his translation differs from the original, while he is forbidden complete translations into his native tongue of writers so eminent as Huysmans and Pierre Louÿs.

Even as regards the novel the difference is marked. Not all the French condemnations of the nineteenth century prevented the Romantic movement from working itself out in a decadence which, however distasteful to some minds, was the logical conclusion of the movement and a necessary phase in the development of European culture. In England the same tendencies were concealed beneath an unhealthy and stultifying hypocrisy. Similarly the French law has failed to stifle new developments in form and subject matter. Of recent times no novel by a writer of established reputation has been legally condemned. The nearest the French have approached to the imbecility of the *Well of Loneliness* prosecution was the pother among the dotards of the Legion of Honour over Victor Margueritte's *La Garçonne*. When the Customs authorities made their mediaeval bonfire of the first edition of James Joyce's *Ulysses* on the quay of Folkestone harbour in 1922, Proust was publishing his great work without let or hindrance. Since that time the modern novel in France has developed into a true mirror of the age. In England, the law and its repercussions in the publishing trade keep the novel in leading-strings. Richard Aldington publishes the full

Above All Liberties

text of his works in the United States and allows "the English to make what cuts their absurd prejudices demand." E. M. Forster and other eminent men of letters have protested bitterly against the law.

With so much similarity, to what can be attributed so great a disparity? It is difficult to find an answer. It is probable that the tradition of European culture has bitten more deeply into the French people than into the English. Certainly liberal education is more diffused than here. Consequently there is a wider respect for letters and for literary freedom. A French author who stands his ground when attacked by the law can at least expect courtesy from his judges and support from his public. There is no place in the civilised world where a man of letters is so scurvily treated as in an English Law Court; and the public are indifferent to his fate. Then there is more solidarity in the literary world of France than in that of England. It is not surprising that our popular press, when at a loss for one of its almost hourly "sensations," should now and then demand the withdrawal of a "disgraceful" book. But it is astonishing that the outcry should be echoed in the columns of a periodical with the reputation of the *Spectator*, as it was over *To Beg I Am Ashamed*; or that the same periodical should incite a police prosecution of a book reviewed in its columns. In France writers rely on verbal weapons when quarrelling over matters of taste unless political

Outrage Aux Mœurs

or patriotic passions are aroused. Finally, the comparative absence of moral hypocrisy from public life engenders a healthier atmosphere. One of the artists whose work in the *Courrier Français* had been twice condemned was awarded the Legion of Honour in 1908. M. Barthou, who presided at the banquet given for the occasion, welcoming "*ce récidiviste de droit commun*," said: "*Je suis heureux de venir, au nom du Gouvernement, réparer les bévues de la magistrature.*" When will an English statesman make similar reparation to the memory of Havelock Ellis?

Whatever may be the true explanation of these differences, there is no doubt that the legal conception of *outrage aux bonnes mœurs*, like the "obscene libel" of English-speaking countries, has the same fundamental origin. It is an expression of the prudery that sprang up with the Industrial Revolution. Society, until that time essentially rural, became predominantly urban. The clear, if somewhat superficial, thinking of the Age of Reason was obscured by an uprush of plebeian superstition, sentimentality and emotionalism. Even the enlightened thought of the nineteenth century, in spite of its scientific triumphs and its victories over religious dogma, was content, with a few brilliant exceptions, to remain essentially theological in its attitude to one of the most important factors in human life. We have already commented on the unfortunate results, cultural and social, of that obscurantism. The cloud seemed to be receding in France before the war.

Above All Liberties

In America it is clearing unmistakably, if more slowly. Those who believe that the good is best sought by way of knowledge and rational discussion will hope that it may soon lift in England.

CHAPTER X

THE PROBLEM OF PORNOGRAPHY

WE have seen how laws against pornography lend themselves to manipulation and extension whereby they become instruments for curtailing freedom of intellectual and aesthetic expression and for limiting discussion and speculation on ethical and social problems. Such laws so developed are arbitrary and unjust in their immediate operation and their scientific, artistic and social repercussions are so deleterious as to far outweigh any good that may be expected of them. The least that can be demanded in any community that calls itself free is that such laws be restricted to their ostensible and original purpose. But this compromise although rendered necessary by present public opinion is bound to be unsatisfactory. The correct and ultimate solution is that the law should cease to concern itself with books which are addressed to educated adults, and that the police should confine their activities to the protection of minors and of those who for one reason or another can reasonably be regarded as *in statu pupillari*. Even here the question is more a matter for parental and educational control than for police action. The police need only be called in to deal with deliberate and persistent subversion of the authority of parents and those

Above All Liberties

in loco parentis. As regards children there is little evidence that sexual writing is harmful: it is generally rejected as of little interest. In the case of adolescents, it may even be beneficial so long as love is depicted as something attractive and beautiful. On the other hand, early and familiar knowledge of violence, cruelty and crime is more than the immature mind can digest. Where these things are associated with eroticism the effect is undoubtedly harmful. I know of no worse reading for juveniles than the average Sunday newspaper.

In addition to the protection of the young, and their like, educated adults may perhaps claim the protection of the law against being forced to see, either by public exhibition or private communication, literary or pictorial matter which is distasteful to them. Beyond these limits no literary or pictorial expression should logically be regarded as either "obscene libel" or "*outrage aux mœurs.*"

But if so far-reaching a reform is to come about some clear thinking on the part of intelligent people is called for. Behind all discussions on this subject looms the bogey of pornography. It is assumed that there is some homogeneous and simple thing called "pornography" and that this thing is morally repudiated *in toto* by all right-minded people. Now the reform advocated above involves a limited toleration of pornography. It does not necessarily imply even a limited approval of pornography. It cannot be too

The Problem of Pornography

often insisted (though it is odd that it should be necessary to do so) that to hold that the suppression of a thing by law does more harm than good, does not mean that one approves of the thing in question. Examples in relation to alcoholic drinks, abortion and homo-sexuality will readily occur to the reader. In this chapter, having agreed that a certain amount of legal toleration of pornography is expedient, I want to ask two questions: What is "pornography"? What should be the attitude of well-disposed people towards the thing (or things) denoted by that word?

The first question at once presents a difficulty. The authorities (if they agree about nothing else) are unanimous that "obscenity" and "pornography" are indefinable terms. Only if we accept the word "obscenity" in the sense assigned to it by Havelock Ellis can we arrive at anything like an objective definition. Ellis says that the obscene is that which is "off the scene" on the stage of life and normally hidden. If we apply this idea to literature, we may say that an "obscene book" is one that at any given time is not permitted to circulate openly by reason of erotic subject matter or manner of treatment of erotic subject matter. The time factor is important because what is obscene to one generation may not be so to another. Ellis's own work was undoubtedly "obscene" in this sense in 1897, just as Edward Charles's *The Sexual Impulse* is "obscene" to-day. If we take an objective view of the matter, condemna-

Above All Liberties

tion by a properly constituted court of law must be a decisive test.

Similarly, withdrawal from circulation by any of the great scholastic libraries constitutes "obscenity" according to this definition. For instance, John Robertson's *Generative System* (1817 and 1824) falls within it. This book is not in the public catalogue of the British Museum Reading Room, and only the most persistent inquiries will establish the existence of a copy in that library. With equal justification John F. W. Meagher's *Masturbation* (1924) will be included together with all other Bodleian books whose press marks are prefixed with the admonitory ϕ. The scarcely less witty $\ni$ (i.e. scruple) of the Boston Athenaeum must similarly mark another collection within the scope of the definition.

The British Museum's practice of excluding certain books from the General Catalogue is a serious matter. Many of the books so excluded are of important literary, historical and scientific interest. The guileless reader who relies on the catalogue is left in complete ignorance of their existence; and, what is more, the value of the published catalogue as a bibliographical work is greatly impaired to the detriment of subscribers all over the world. The system of the library of Congress is vastly superior. *No book is omitted* from the author catalogue. As the Library is open to any person over sixteen, however, certain books are locked up and only issued at the discretion of the

The Problem of Pornography

Superintendent. There are no rules, but it is probable that many books would be refused to young persons and women warned as to their character. But it can be definitely stated that no serious investigator, male or female, would be refused material however "obscene," and that full information is available to all as to what the library contains on any subject. The position at the London Library is similarly more favourable. Although special application must be made to obtain certain books "in the Librarian's room," they are all included in the catalogue. A catalogue of the "Enfer" of the Bibliothèque Nationale was published in 1913. Before leaving the subject of great libraries, it is worthy of note that during Hume's librarianship of the Advocates' Library in Edinburgh two of the Governors ordered the collection to be purged of La Fontaine's *Contes* and two other French books. They have since been replaced.

To return to our definition, we must also include books whose circulation has been restricted for erotic reasons such as Payne's translation of *Villon*, Grose's *Dictionary*, and Boccaccio's *Decameron*. Payne's *Villon* (1878–92) was published "for private circulation only" and has never been publicly issued in this country, although a reprint was issued in New York in 1918. When Grose's *Dictionary* was reprinted in 1931 it was deemed prudent to publish it privately. Complete translations of the *Decameron* have always been privately published, or highly priced, in this country until quite recently, when an American reprint of Payne's translation (without his notes) appeared in the London bookshops. Interesting as this definition is, and useful as it may be for, say, bibliographical purposes, it gives little help in arriving at an understanding of what people mean when they use the word "obscene" in a morally reprehensible sense.

If we turn to the word "pornographic" the position is no better. Literally the word means "descriptive of harlotry"; but the most strait-laced Puritan would hardly describe Sanger's *History of Prostitution* as pornographic, though I have always felt that the author's chilly soul warmed a little when describing the "better class" brothels of New York. Most frequently "pornographic" is equated with "sexually stimulating." But this is hopelessly subjective. What stimulates one person will not stimulate another. The statement "Book A stimulated person B" tells us far more about B than A. Then this definition generally implies that sexual stimulation is always and everywhere undesirable which surely is not so. In this relation I must differ from those opponents of obscenity laws who claim that if certain books are found to be sexually stimulating it is because the people who read them are afflicted by some moral defect or "impurity." I suppose that the majority of men and women are capable of being stimulated by some book in some circumstances, and are not for

The Problem of Pornography

that reason particularly blameworthy; nor, as I shall suggest at the end of this chapter, is the fact at all times and in all places to be deplored. This fact must be honestly faced. Nevertheless, when books are blamed for evil consequences and anti-social conduct, the fault is generally with the reader rather than the book and it would be absurd to attempt to suppress a book because it was proved to have had an undesirable effect on an unbalanced person. I suppose the most dreadful indictment ever made against a book was written by Gilles de Rais, the companion in arms of Joan of Arc. After her death he fell into evil ways and was ultimately tried for a series of sadistic child murders committed in his various châteaux. He confessed; before his execution he addressed an appeal to Charles VII relating how he was corrupted in youth, and containing the following passage:

Estant d'aventure, dans la librairie dûdit chateau je trouvai un livre latin de la vie et des mœurs des Césars de Rome, par un savant historien qui a nom Suetonius; ledit livre était orné d'images fort bien peintes, auxquelles se voyaient les déportements de ces empereurs païens, et je lu en cette belle histoire comment Tiberius, Caracolla et autres Césars s'esbattaient avec des enfants et prenaient singulier plaisir à les martyriser. Sur quoi, je voulus imiter les dits Césars et, le même soir, je commencai à ce faire en suivant les images de la leçon et du livre.

It is only necessary to observe that multitudes of men must have read Suetonius without any ill effects

Above All Liberties

whatever. Perhaps the nearest we can get to a definition of pornography is writing or drawing executed with the *intention* of exciting sexuality and without a sense of moral responsibility. But this is entirely unsatisfactory, for who is to look into the mind of the author? We may be sure that the censorial will always see there what their prejudices dictate; and that nothing stimulates prejudice so much as novelty.

We had better leave this matter of definition, and approach our second task of forming an opinion about "pornography" by taking seriatim certain classes of writing to which the term has been applied with something like common consent.

I

First of all let us take the sort of books which were dealt with in a notorious prosecution which resulted in the imprisonment of a Charing Cross Road bookseller in 1933. The *Times* of April 30th gives their titles: *The Autobiography of a Flea, Flossie, The Way of a Man with a Maid*. The case excited a great deal of attention because the police employed an *agent provocateur* who posed as an Army officer and visited the shop six times before he persuaded the bookseller to break the law by selling the books. It is important, in justice to the police, to emphasise that this case differs very widely from cases where the "obscenity" laws are invoked against reputable authors. Whether

The Problem of Pornography

the difference justifies the conduct of the police the reader must decide for himself. Almost invariably books of this character are written with a minimum of literary competence, badly printed, and shoddily produced. Sometimes, not always, they quite fail to fulfil the expectations aroused by their titles and appearance, and are in the nature of a catch-penny fraud. In either case, they are designed to extract money from people with an unhealthy curiosity and with a hunger for sexual experience of any sort.

The existence of this kind of thing is surely symptomatic of the deplorable state of education in this country. Any reasonable measure of sex education would do away with the morbid curiosity which creates the demand for these books and would soon lead to the abolition of those extremities of sex starvation which lead people to take pleasure in such trash.

II

There is another sort of pornography against which charges of literary incompetence and trashiness cannot always be sustained. It arises from the circumstances that (as a certain school of modern sexologists are never tired of telling us) the association of the sexual impulse with such emotions as love, tenderness and creativeness is not a necessary one. It is quite possible for it to be disentangled from these things and to stand alone in a sort of reptilian isolation and coldness

Above All Liberties

sufficient unto itself. Books have been written which concern themselves with the physical side of sex and nothing else. Limited by the essential simplicity of their subject, they consist of a wearisome series of episodes fundamentally similar. Anxious to give value for money, the author repeats himself endlessly. In a vain endeavour to escape this imposed monotony he attempts fantastic variations which achieve only the ludicrous. The author has rarely the wit to be critical of the morality he outrages, but takes a childish "naughty-naughty" delight in flaunting it. Sometimes he cloaks his purpose under a hypocritical pretence of exposing the vices of his time in order to improve them. This "gallant" pornography, as we may term it, was rife in eighteenth-century France. A large collection of this literature made by Gaston Camus at the time of the Revolution is now housed in the Palais Bourbon.

It is illuminating to compare this type of literature with *The Arabian Nights* now that Burton's translation (the only satisfactory one) is less inaccessible than it used to be. The narrator of the stories that make up the *Nights* has no inhibitions about sex. When he comes to the subject he treats it frankly, and is quite willing to laugh or weep over it according to the tenor of his tale. At the same time there is none of the monotony which we have seen to be a characteristic of "gallant" literature. Neither is the narrator obsessed with the subject or furtive about it. It occupies about

The Problem of Pornography

the same amount of space and attention among the adventures and wonders of the tales as it does in real life. I do not suggest that *The Arabian Nights* is a standard on which European literature should model itself. We must expect taste as to what is "on the scene" and what is "off the scene" to vary from people to people, from place to place, and from time to time. But the matter is one of *taste* and not one suitable for the jurisdiction of judge and policeman. The reputable writer is most amenable to opinion which he respects. The disreputable scribbler who seeks to turn a dishonest penny by outraging the sensibilities of the public should in any healthy community be treated with contempt—and nothing more.

Indeed "gallant" literature seems worthy of neither very serious attention nor very solemn denunciation. Some adolescents experience a passing attraction for it—a sort of literary measles—but they grow out of the phase. Deprived of "bootleg" value, the older examples would become literary curiosities and modern manifestations poor rivals to the detective story and the thriller[1] and such comparatively harmless if unedifying ephemeras of literature.

III

But the process which results in "gallant" pornography can be taken a step farther. Not only can the

[1] "I wonder why murder is considered less immoral than fornication in literature."—GEORGE MOORE.

Above All Liberties

sexual impulse be isolated, it can be re-associated with cruel, harsh and destructive emotions. It is this psychological association, rather than the physical deviation of the impulse from its normal object, which I regard as the really significant characteristic of the sexuality of which de Sade was the arch-prophet; although this type of pornography is almost inevitably concerned with deviations. There is an unholy galaxy of lesser writers of the same sort coming down to such magazines as the "Crenome" and the "Pearl" which were published in London in the middle of the last century. To this pornography the French word *maudite* is applicable.

It forms an intractable kernel to the pornography problem. What are we to think about it? To any ordinary mind it is revolting. Few people would like to see it in the hands of the general public. At the same time the present position is far from satisfactory. When written by a man of the ability of de Sade this type of pornography has a certain legitimate interest not only to the alienist and the sexological specialist but to the literary man. Several books about de Sade have been openly published during the present century; and innumerable references to him and his work are made in current literature. Aldous Huxley, for example, devotes some pages of *Ends and Means* to de Sade. This is a great change since the last century, when his name could not be printed; and Swinburne pulled the editor of the *Spectator's* leg gloriously with

The Problem of Pornography

reviews of works by Felicien Cossu and Ernest Cloriet into one of which he dragged condemnatory reference to the Great Unmentionable. Unhappily the imaginary nature both of the French authors and their depraved works was discovered just in time to prevent publication.[1] It is probable that it was a perusal of copies of de Sade's writings from the library of Monckton Milnes that fanned Swinburne's spirit into the incandescence which gave the world *Poems and Ballads* and *Songs Before Sunrise*. But if to-day we are allowed to discuss de Sade, it is a little silly that no one is supposed to see the books that all the talk is about. A modern edition of de Sade's works edited from original manuscripts by Maurice Heine was published in Paris during the thirties.

The regrettable phenomenon of this type of pornography can be put down to a very large extent to unwise and obscurantist treatment of sexual matters, particularly to our savage and tribal attitude to deviations. With proper sex education, more reasonable sexual customs, and a scientific attitude to sexual pathology, it would, I believe, tend to disappear. What little remained would be regarded in a very different light than at present. It would lose the value that always attached itself to the forbidden and the taboo. Many people to-day who treasure examples of this type of literature on out-of-the-way shelves of their libraries would probably be less proud of it if it

[1] Printed in booklet form 1915 and 1916.

Above All Liberties

were condemned, not by law, but by a healthy public opinion. It is repellent rather than harmful to the normal mind, and a definite gain would be effected if it were taken out of the "hush-hush" atmosphere in which it breeds and acquires an exaggerated importance.

How ineffective is force to suppress even the most unattractive activities of the human mind is manifest if we look beneath the surface into popular mentality. There have recently appeared on the bookstalls cheap editions of American "thrillers" in relation to which the judgment passed above on this type of literature is too mild. The books of one author in particular are exclusively devoted to violence, cruelty and salacity— in short, dilute de Sade. If the undiluted mixture were better known some readers might not be so complacent about them. At any rate their popularity (over fifty thousand copies of one gangster novel have been sold) is evidence of the uselessness of censorship as an educational process. Again, there is in private possession in this country a collection of transcriptions of contemporary cloacal graphitae made by a historian and sexologist of repute now deceased. It consists of about five thousand examples each written on an index card bearing the place and date of the inscription. The cards have been scientifically classified according to the activity described or referred to by the inscription. I have had an opportunity to examine the collection and I think that it is safe to say that there is scarcely

The Problem of Pornography

a form of sexual activity, normal or deviated, solitary, dual or concerted, known to either the modern or the ancient world which is not represented. For the most part the writers treat hetero- and homo-sexuality with an equal absence of moral responsibility. They have no respect for law or custom, and merely deplore as unfortunate or unjust any police action they may mention. Of course the writers are a limited class. But the evidence is that they are not a haphazard collection of abnormals. Certainly they are not illiterate, but show signs of elementary education and Cockney intelligence. I believe them to be fairly representative of Central London residents of the depressed classes who can be seen any evening wandering the streets, queuing for cheap cinemas, and haunting the pin saloons. Their state of mind results from the sexual ignorance and deprivation which authority attempts to force on them.

A special class of sadistic literature is constituted by books appealing pre-eminently to flagellomania. In its milder forms this sub-class does not merit the severe condemnation proper to books devoted to the grosser forms of sadism. Much of it is so silly as to be merely risible, and some of it, in spite of dubious motives for publication, has genuine historical interest. On the Continent flagellomania is known as *le vice Anglais*, and there seems to be some justification for the idea that it is particularly prevalent in this country. Certainly England has lagged behind the rest of the civilised world in its attitude to penal flogging and pedagogic and domestic chastisement. During the last century James Camden Hotten was responsible for a number of publications dealing with flagellation of varying degrees of respectability. One of them, a history of flagellation, written by James G. Bertram (the author of *The Harvest of the Sea*) under a clerical pseudonym, still continues a popular and inglorious career in the less reputable bookshops. Others of these books of Hotten's were issued in a grandiloquent series called the "Library Illustrative of Social Progress from the Original Editions collected by the late Henry Thomas Buckle, Author of 'A History of Civilization in England'." Both the description and the alleged derivation of the copy were equally bogus.

IV

It will be a relief to turn from the distressing manifestations made by sadistic literature of human degeneracy to a type of publication at the other end of the pornographic scale. This type of publication has of recent years been produced in large quantities in America. There it generally takes the form of some work by a reputable sexologist, reprinted (and probably pirated) in a tawdry, meretricious and journalistic fashion, with sensational and inflammatory headlines and (perhaps) illustrations which did not appear in the original edition and have little or no relevance to

The Problem of Pornography

the text. The text is often corrupt and even bowdlerised. Much fuss is made about "limited editions" and "private circulation," although the publishers are only too anxious to sell to anyone misguided enough to pay the exorbitant price demanded.

The most impudent example of this type of literary catch-penny was published in New York under the title *The 120 Days of Sodom*, the author being given as de Sade. Both this title and author appeared on the cover and the price was very high. In fact the book was a reprint of one published at the beginning of the present century by Iwan Bloch, in which he deals with his discovery of the manuscript of de Sade's *Cent et Vingt jours de Sodom* and with the subject of de Sade's time more generally.

In 1937 Sir Edward Tindal Atkinson, Director of Public Prosecutions, published an exposition of the law of obscene libel in pamphlet form,[1] in which he complained of the increase in recent years of "books which, while masquerading under the guise of scientific works, purport in extreme detail to lay before the public the subject of sexual relations and aberrations." This passage caused some indignation as it was thought to refer to the work of serious though unorthodox sexological writers. I was informed, however, that he was not referring to English writers, but to precisely the bogus American publications we are considering.

[1] *Obscene Literature in Law and Practice* (London: Christophers).

Above All Liberties

During the latter half of the last century, when the law of "obscene libel" became a serious menace to the free circulation of ideas on sexual subjects in this country, a regular trade in books of this character in English sprang up on the Continent. The publisher Lisieux specialised in historical and literary works of an erotic character. Later Carrington carried on a similar trade, adding scientific works on sex to his lists. No exception could be taken to the way in which the publications of these houses were produced and edited. They were well printed, scholarly and often of considerable historical or scientific interest. But it is safe to assert that the motive which actuated the purchasers was rarely unalloyed zeal for historical or scientific knowledge. In our own time some of the Carrington books were reprinted in England by the Fortune Press. All went well for some years, but in 1934 the publishers were prosecuted[1] and a holocaust made of all their publications of this type and many others. Among them was the Carrington Petronius, the only complete and unbowdlerised translation of the *Satyricon* into English. It was a most scholarly edition, with very full notes, and the Fortune Press reprint went unmolested for seven years. I notice that an American reprint of this same translation of the *Satyricon* (without the notes) was recently sold in the London bookshops at a low price.

Quite clearly this phenomenon of books of his-

[1] The case is described in my *The Banned Books of England*.

torical interest, and of books by reputable scientific authors, appearing in the guise of pornography (I would put it that way and not, as Sir Edward Tindal Atkinson does, the other way round) is due to the fact that their normal circulation is interfered with by the law. To take one example, Iwan Bloch's *Das Sexualleben unserer Zeit* was translated into English faithfully and in a scholarly manner and published in the normal way as a scientific work in 1909. It was prosecuted and condemned. As a result no more of Bloch's books have been translated into English in the same scholarly way; and his works are one of the mines industriously worked by the meretricious American publishers whose products we have dealt with. The treatment of his *Geschlechtsleben* is worthy of special note. No scholarly translation exists. Abridged translations have been made in which it is impossible to tell where matter has been omitted and where the author has been departed from. There is an American edition of the sort I have described bound up with an awe-inspiring "Secret Cabinet" of plates —bad reproductions of Rowlandson, Gillray, etc. The original German is quite unsensational in its format. I may say that it betrays in an exaggerated form both the virtues and the vices of German scholarship. It is a mass of exact and painstaking information about English social life, literature and art: yet the author entirely fails to see the wood for the trees, and his interpretation of his laboriously

Above All Liberties

collected material presents a grotesquely false picture of English life. One cannot expect the English to feel flattered when flagellomania is put forward as their main preoccupation and the simulation of virginity the chief object of their medical skill: but that is no reason for refusing to profit from the results of Bloch's exceedingly able and valuable factual research.

In the period between the end of the war of 1914–1918 and the Nazi revolution, the great German sexologists like Bloch and Hirschfeld found a host of imitators and populariser in their native country. Their books, often profusely illustrated, would be dubbed as pornography by many people, and in some cases the integrity of either author or publisher must appear to an unprejudiced mind at least open to doubt.

v

Next we come to the simple question of vocabulary. Writing is classed as pornography merely because it uses plain, homely words in relation to the natural functions and anatomy of the body instead of Latinised words or circumlocutions. D. H. Lawrence did a great deal to counteract this stupid idea. This country still bans his *Lady Chatterley's Lover* in its unexpurgated form; but I believe it will soon be published in America. We have recently had published in London a modern English version of Chaucer in which the

The Problem of Pornography

poet's vocabulary is not disguised; and in an American translation Villon's vocabulary is represented (as it should be) by the English vernacular. Some years ago Janet Chance, the author of *The Cost of English Morals* (1931), conducted an interesting investigation into the vocabulary used in the home and nursery by those who visited her Sex Education Centre.

Plain language is no evidence of coarse ideas. Nor, on the other hand, is a refined vocabulary any guarantee of refined thought. This is illustrated by a literary *tour de force* of the last century. Shortly after the Revolution of 1830 there was a dinner party of brilliant young men at a Parisian restaurant. The talk ran from politics to literature, from literature in general to erotic literature in particular. The licence allowed to the ancient writers was compared with the restraints under which the French novelists of the time were becoming restive. The question arose whether these restraints could be loosened without damaging the elegance of French diction. Was the genius of the French language capable of dealing with the situation? An elegant young man just out of his teens who had been yawning most of the time suddenly became attentive. Would the company put the matter to the test by meeting in the same place in a few days' time? He would see what he could do. At the agreed rendezvous the young man (said to have been Alfred de Musset) produced the manuscript of *Gamiani*, a work second to none in licence but without one coarse word or expression throughout its length. The aptness of the French language in this *genre* is illustrated (on a much higher plane of artistic merit) in some of the *Contes* of La Fontaine.

VI

Another type of writing is condemned as pornographic because it is humorous about sexual subjects. The idea is that sex is somehow "sacred" and an inappropriate subject for laughter, let alone humour or wit. The truth is, of course, that men have always made jokes about the things they have taken most seriously. Blasphemous jokes are losing their appeal to the modern mind not because we are more pious than our fathers, but because we are ceasing to believe that organised religion is either awe-inspiring or important. Throughout our lives we are continually advancing from one state of consciousness to another. A baby takes an equal and undifferentiated interest and delight in all its bodily functions. At an early date it realises that some of these functions meet with social approval and others not. To some extent it must suppress its interest and delight in those things which are not pleasing to its elders. The suppressed matter is soon forgotten but it still exists in the sub-conscious mind. This process goes on till the mind is like a stratified portion of the earth's crust. But even the lowest levels of mental experience, although forgotten

The Problem of Pornography

and unconscious, are by no means inactive. From time to time the ideas embodied in them find their way to the surface of consciousness. They have various ways of doing this. One is through dreams. Another through humour. Humour is psychologically beneficial and in our society its beneficial nature is recognised, and a sense of humour is considered a necessary part of a well-balanced mental make-up—in every department of life except that of sex and its physically associated functions.

The Greeks took a different view. They prized the balanced life above everything. In their dramatic festivals, after the tragedy with its preoccupation with exalted and religious motives, came the comedies which gave rein to obscenity and coarseness of every description. "Obscenity," as Ellis says, is that which is normally "off-the-scene" of life. The Greeks thought it well for mental health that it should on occasion be brought on the scene. The actors of the mediaeval moralities and miracle plays acted on the same principles. Modern psychology suggests that the principle is a right one, and that the attitude was far more healthy than that of a famous translator of the Greek, Professor Gilbert Murray. I have nothing but admiration for his work, considered as English poetry, but as a reflection of the meaning of the original it can only be described as priggish. *The Frogs* is roaring farce and satire combined, in which the grossest coarseness is mingled with knife-edge wit

Above All Liberties

and humorous wisdom. Yet in Murray's translation "to break wind" becomes "to blow one's nose," and even mention of "backside" is suppressed.

If the Greeks were right in this attitude we need not take too solemn a view of the obscenity of modern society as evidenced by smoking-room stories, limericks and the vaudeville stage. All we need ask is that such pleasantries be reserved for their proper time and place. The non-stop retailer of improprieties is as big a bore as the sour-faced Puritan. Obscenity that is not novel and occasional is unbelievably dreary. Whether any useful purpose is achieved by committing the spoken jest to print as was done in a collection of limericks privately published under the name of Norman Douglas in the early twenties is a matter of taste, but there is no reason why humorous writing should not deal with sex as much as with anything else. The incongruities and paradoxes which run through all this bewildering universe certainly do not avoid the manifestation of human love.

VII

Lastly, we come to a type of book common in Classical times, prominent in Oriental literature, and not unknown in Europe at the Renaissance: the well-written erotic book, designed by some master of his craft to instruct in, *and stimulate to*, sexual activity. Such books are a marked contrast to our chilly and

The Problem of Pornography

clinical manuals of sex instruction. No type of book would be more unhesitatingly dubbed "pornographic" by those who make free with this term.

The objection to erotic books in Western civilisation rests, first on the fiction that the sex act is instinctive in civilised humans (which it is not), and secondly on the idea that unless love is made very dull there will be a great deal too much of it. The result of this attitude is that many a love affair culminates in a furtive fumbling under bed-clothes and the semi-rape of a half-stifled woman. I think that the real offence of Edward Charles's *The Sexual Impulse* was that of its being written *con amore* and spiced with humour. Charles held the view that the time had come to discard that specially solemn style always assumed by Victorians when speaking and writing of sex, and which Havelock Ellis, perforce, adopted to some extent. If one's sex instruction is always solemn and even sanctimonious, is not one likely to be dull in love, where gaiety, variety and joy should abound? Charles addressed a book of sex instruction to educated adults. He is scientific, literary, gay—and even witty at the expense of certain traditional superstitions. The traditionalists do not argue—they dub his book pornography.

Our society allows any amount of sexual stimulation at all times by poster, newspaper, cinema, theatre, and women's dress in public; but it frowns on sexual satisfaction and aids thereto. In the society of the

Above All Liberties

future (if indeed men are advancing to a better world) I believe that this emphasis will be reversed. Life will be less sex-obsessed but, at proper times and seasons, physical love will be restored to its ancient dignity, variety and gaiety. Both modesty and the art of love will come into their own again. In that society the erotic book, we may expect, will play a part.

I am aware that in this chapter I have gone far beyond what is likely to be found popularly acceptable or to become practicable politics for some time. For the present the most that we can hope is that the evils which we have seen result to science, literature, art and society from obscenity laws will be mitigated by an honest endeavour to restrict the operation of those laws to their avowed purpose, namely, the suppression of pornography. In addition a few minor reforms may be possible. Sealed postal packages the outside of which give no offence and the contents of which raise no complaint from the receiver should surely be free of the law. Also it is not unreasonable to expect that private publication to groups of responsible persons should be left alone.

But it is important that thoughtful and intelligent people should look farther ahead than what is immediately practicable and face the problem of pornography (which is the root of the trouble) in a clearheaded way. For an attempt to restrict the law to its

The Problem of Pornography

avowed purpose can never be more than partially successful. Our old and grey rulers and governors will always see the spectre of "pornography" in any sexual ideas that are either novel or entertaining. The law will always be twisted to penalise the free expression of opinion. So long as we chase the bogey of "pornography" we cannot be, we cannot expect to be, a free and civilised community. Pornography-hunting is no more consistent with civilisation than witch-hunting, to which it bears a close psychological resemblance. We must lay the ghost by clear thinking, education and the improvement of manners.

This is the only fundamental cure for the evil which has formed the subject of this book. We have seen that literary "obscenity" laws have their ideological roots in the far-off ages of ecclesiastical government and superstition. We have seen how the legal control of sexual expression faded away before the spread of enlightenment which flowed from the Renaissance. Then we have seen how a judge-made law of "obscene libel" grew up almost from nothing. First it is invoked against gross and public breaches of good taste. It is fortified by legislation and further judicial decisions. It becomes an engine for curbing intellectual speculation and for obstructing the education of the people. It no longer confines itself to writings addressed to the general public, but concerns itself with publications addressed to restricted groups, and even with communications between individuals. Of its very

Above All Liberties

nature its operation is arbitrary and a negation of law properly described. We have studied the direct evils of this state of affairs, and we have traced its far-reaching repercussions. We have examined similar phenomena abroad. The resulting picture is a disturbing one. It has been treated too lightly by liberals who assumed too readily that the victory for freedom of thought over authoritarianism and obscurantism had been won. It is a matter which deserves the attention of all liberty-loving people at a time when that freedom is attacked on all sides; when the forces of ecclesiasticism and reaction are everywhere in the ascendant and ready to seize on any weapon to farther their cause. Such attention is the more urgent when we realise that the solution of society's sexual and biological problems is of primary importance if our civilisation is to survive.

BIBLIOGRAPHY

NOTE.—Many of the following books cover much wider ground than the chapter under which they appear. I have listed them where they have been most useful to me. I have not repeated items contained in the Bibliography to my *The Banned Books of England.*

CHAPTER I

The Literary Policy of the Church of Rome, by Joseph Mendham (2nd edition, London, 1830). Mus. Brit. 1123 k.4

Books Condemned to be Burnt, by James Anson Farrer (London, 1892)

Sir Charles Sedley, by V. de Sola Pinto (London, 1927)

Social Control of Sex Expression, by Geoffrey May (London, 1930; New York, 1931)

Index Librorum Prohibitorum (Typis Polyglottis Vaticanis, 1938). Mus. Brit. 11914. f. 9

CHAPTER II

A History of the Booksellers, by Henry Curwen (Guildford) [1873]

The Unspeakable Curll, Bookseller; to which is added a full list of his books, by Ralph Strauss (London : New York: 1927)

Above All Liberties

CHAPTER III

"Comic Dramatists of the Restoration" (1841) in Lord Macaulay's *Critical and Historical Essays*

Sex Expression in Literature, by Victor Francis Calverton (New York, 1926)

Liberty in the Modern State, by Harold J. Laski (London: Toronto: 1930); with a new introduction (London, Penguin, 1937)

Hold Your Tongue! Adventures in Libel and Slander, by Morris L. Ernst and Alexander Lindey (New York, 1932); with an introduction by A. P. Herbert (London: Toronto: 1936)

Mrs. Grundy in Scotland, by Willa Muir (London, 1936)

Les Crises de la Morale et de la Moralité dans l'Histoire de la Civilisation et de la Littérature des Pays Anglo-Saxons, by Paul Yvon (Paris, 1937)

The Athanæum: A Mirror of Victorian Culture, by Leslie A. Marchand (University of North Carolina, 1941)

CHAPTER IV

Sonnets and Folk Songs from the Spanish, by Havelock Ellis (London and Boston, 1925)

Havelock Ellis, by Isaac Goldberg (New York and London, 1926)

My Life, by Havelock Ellis (London, 1940)

Inside the Whale, by George Orwell (London, 1940)
    Contains a critique of *The Tropic of Cancer* and Henry Miller's other work.

Bibliography

CHAPTER V

Whited Sepulchres, being an account of my trial and imprisonment for a parody of Verlaine and some other verses, by Count Potocki of Montalk (London, *Right Review*, 1936)

Verlaine, poète saturnien, by Marcel Coulon (Paris, 1929). Translated by Edgell Rickword (London, 1932)

CHAPTER VII

Sex in Civilisation, edited by V. F. Culverton and S. D. Schmalhausen (New York: London: 1929), particularly the Essay "Sex Censorship and Democracy" by Waldo Frank.

CHAPTER VIII

A Diary in America, by Captain Frederick Marryat (London, 1839)

Dirty Hands, or the True-Born Censor, by R. P. Blackmur (Minority Pamphlet No. 5, Cambridge, 1930)

Mrs. Grundy, a history of four centuries of morals intended to illuminate present problems in Great Britain and the United States, by Leo Markun (New York and London, 1930)

Sex in the Arts. A Symposium edited by John Francis McDermott and Kendall B. Taft (New York, 1932), particularly the essay "Sex and Censorship" by Morris L. Ernst.

Above All Liberties

Only Yesterday. An informal history of the 1920s in America, by Frederick Lewis Allen (New York and London, 1931: London, *Penguin*, 1938)

The Fruits of Philosophy, by Charles Knowlton, edited with an introductory notice by Norman E. Himes (Mount Vernon, 1937)

British Museum Paper: Magistrate's decision in *The World I Never Made* case (State of New York *v.* Vanguard Press). 1937, Mus. Brit. Cup 1247.i.33

A Challenge to Sex Censors, by Theodore Schroeder (New York, privately printed to promote the aims of the Free Speech League, 1938)

The Censor Marches On. Recent Milestones in the Administration of the Obscenity Law in the United States, by Morris L. Ernst and Alexander Lindey (New York, 1940)

CHAPTER IX

Bibliographie des Ouvrages Rélatifs à l'Amour, etc., by M. le Cte D'I*** (*pseud.* of Jules Gay), 3rd edition, 6 vols. (Turin, 1871–3), 4th edition, 4 vols. (Paris, 1894–1900). Mus. Brit. 11903. b.35 and 011902.1.25

Catalogue des Ouvrages Condamnés comme contraire à la morale publique et aux bonnes mœurs du 1er Janvier, 1814 *et* 31 *Décembre*, 1873 (Paris, 1874). Mus. Brit. 11900. aaa.32(3)

Les Procès littéraires au XIXe Siècle, by Alexander Zevaès (2nd edition, Paris, 1924)

The Background of Modern French Literature, by C. H. C. Wright (Boston, 1926)

Bibliography

L'Outrage aux Mœurs, by Lionel D'Autrec (5th edition, Paris, 1929)

La Carne, la Morte e il Diavolo nella Letteratura Romantica, by Mario Praz (Milan, 1930). Translated by Angus Davidson under the title *The Romantic Agony* (London, 1933)

The Erotic History of France, by Henry L. Marchand (New York, 1933)

CHAPTER X

Index Librorum Prohibitorum, Centuria Librorum Absconditorum, and *Catena Librorum Tacendorum*, by Pisanus Fraxi (*pseud.* of Henry Spencer Ashbee) (London, privately printed, 1877, 1879, 1885). Mus. Brit. P.C. 18 b.9

Bibliotheca Arcana seu Catalogus Librorum Penetralium, being brief notices of books that have been secretly printed, prohibited by law, seized, anathematised, burnt or bowdlerised, by Speculator Morum (*pseud.* of Rev. John B. McClellan, who appears to have written Preface. Compiled by Sir William Laird Clowes) (London, 1885). Mus. Brit. P.C. 29.a.5

"The Taboos of the British Museum," by E. S. P. Haynes (*English Review*, December 1913)

Cato or the Future of Censorship, by William Seagle (To-day and To-morrow Series, London and New York, 1930)

Art and Morality, by Oliver de Selincourt (London, 1935)

INDEX

Acton, Mr. Justice, 79
Advocate's Library, Edinburgh, 167
Affirmations, 57
Agents provocateurs, 125, 170–171
Aldington, Richard, 102, 105, 159
Almost Fourteen, 123
America, 97, 120–136, 162, 178
American Tragedy, 125
Answer, The, 121
Arabian Nights, 172–173
Areopagitica, 18
Aristophanes, 126, 185–186
Art of Love, 132
Ascham, Roger, 17
Athenaeum, 38
Atkinson, Sir Edward Tindal, 179, 181
Attentat aux mœurs, 138
Aurevilly, Barbery d', 152
Australia, 46–51, 121
Authors, 15, 25, 97, 149
Autobiography of a Child, 69
Autour d'un Clocher, 153–154

Balzac, Honoré de, 14, 70, 126
Barbier, Mon., 143
Barrin, Abbé, 30
Baudelaire, Charles, 148–150
Bedborough, George, 58–60, 91
Bedborough Trial, 59
Behn, Aphra, 36–37
Belgium, 141, 152–155
Belloc, Hilaire, 16

Béranger, Pierre Jean de, 146, 147, 148
Bérenger, Réné, 139, 140, 142–143
Bertram, James G., 178
Besant, Annie, 91 (*see also under* Bradlaugh)
Bessie Cotter, 118
Bible, 128
Bibliothèque Nationale, 145, 153, 167
Birrell, Augustine, 38
Birth Control—
American law, 131–132
French law, 140–141
(*See also* 51, 68 *and under* Bradlaugh)
Blackham, Robert J., 83
Blasphemous libel, 22, 36
Bloch, Iwan, 134, 179, 181–182
Boccaccio, 14–15, 126, 146, 167–168
Bodkin, Sir Archibald, 89, 141
Bodleian Library, 166
Bonnaire, Henry, 98
Bonnetain, Paul, 154
Bootle Public Library, 105
Boston, 124–125
Boston Athenaeum, 166
Boucher, François, 143
Boulanger, General, 155
Boy, 102
Bradlaugh, Charles, 42, 71–72, 115, 123
Brantôme, 47
Brend, William A., 100–101
British Broadcasting Corporation, 109

197

British Empire, 121
British Museum, 11, 108, 166
Britton, Lionel, 97
Buckle, Henry Thomas, 178
Burton, Sir Richard, 172

Campbell, Lord Chief Justice, 39
Camus, Gaston, 172
Carlyle, Thomas, 146
Carmichael, Alexander, 41
Carpenter, Edward, 53, 65
Carrington, Charles, 180
Casanova, 126, 150
Casanova's Homecoming, 123
Case of Seduction . . . against the Rev. Abbé des Rues, 31, 33
Censorship Act, 18, 21
Censorship of Publications Act, 16
Certiorari, 115
Chance, Janet, 102, 183
"Chanson de la Braguette," 78–79
Chanson des Gueux, 151
Charitable Surgeon, 26
Charles IX, 145
Charles, Edward (*see under* Sexual Impulse)
Charlot s' amuse, 154
Chartroule, Marie Amélie, 152
Chaucer, 78, 81, 93, 128
Chidley, W. J., 121
Church (*see under* Ecclesiastical attitude)
Church Assembly, 132
Cladel, Léon, 152
Clarke, Donald Henderson, 124
Clarke, Sir Percival, 91
Class distinction, 66, 72–73, 101–107, 133

Classics (*see under* Translations)
Cockburn, Lord Chief Justice, 41, 115
Coital technique, 103, 121, 186–187
Common law, 34, 39–41, 189
Comstock, Anthony, 123, 127, 131
Comstock Act, 131
Confessional Unmasked, 39–40
Congress, Library of, 166–167
Connolly, Cyril, 97
Contes Drolatiques, 70
Contraception (*see under* Birth Control)
Corneille, 150
Corneille-Blessebois, Pierre, 152
Council for Investigation of Vatican Influence and Censorship, 16
Council of Trent, 15
Country Life, 84
Courrier Français, 156, 161
Cousins, Sheila, 111–120
Couvray, Louvet de, 146
Crébillon *fils*, 146
Criminal, The, 55
Criminal Justice Bill (1933), 67–68
Cupidon, 156
Curlicism Displayed, 28
Curll, Edmund, 25–35
Curran, Hon. Henry M., 127–130
Customs authorities, 70, 98, 100, 125–127, 131–132, 135–136

Daily Chronicle, 59
Daily Express, 110
Daily Mail, 111–115

Index

Daily Mirror, 112–115
Dance of Life, 61, 121
Daphnis and Chloë, 126
Daudet, Alphonse, 154
De la Mare, Walter, 92
De Rutzen, Sir Albert, 69
Death of a Hero, 102, 105
Decameron (see under Boccaccio)
Deeping, Warwick, 124
Defamatory libel, 22
Definition of "obscenity," 10, 34, 141–145, 165–170
Defoe, 28–29, 30, 126
Dell, Floyd, 97
Delorme, Hugues, 156
Descaves, Lucien, 155
Despised and Rejected, 22
Desprez, Louis, 153–154
Distributing agents, literary, 98–99, 100
Divinités Génératrices, 147
Dominions, British, 121
Douglas, James, 110
Douglas, Norman, 186
Dreiser, Theodore, 97, 125
Drolleries, 21
Drysdale, George, 48
Duluare, Antoine Jacques, 147
Dumas père et fils, 14

Ecclesiastical attitude, 13–16, 23, 39, 80, 133, 189, 190
Ecclesiastical Courts, 13, 16, 18
Education for Christian Marriage, 132
Eighteenth century, 25, 36, 145, 146
Eire, 16
Eldon, Lord, 91
Elements of Social Science, 48

Eliot, T. S., 49, 70, 85, 92
Ellis, Henry Havelock, 43–74, 91, 161, 165, 185, 187
Elmer Gantry, 124
Ends and Means, 174
Épaves, Les, 150
Ernst, Morris, 127
Ervine, St. John, 124
Esher, Lord, 92
Essex, Walter Devereux 1st Earl of, 29
Eymery, Marguerite, 153
Eyqueum, Albert, 142, 143

Faber, Geoffrey, 10
Fabian Society, 52
Falstaff Press, 134
Farrell, James T., 127–131
Fate of Homo Sapiens, 15–16
Faublas, Amours du Chevalier de, 146
"Fellowship of the New Life," 52, 55
Female, 124
Féré, Charles, 60
Feuchtwanger, Leon, 124
Fèvre, Henri, 153
Fielding, Henry, 128
Fifteen Plagues of a Maidenhead, 23
Film censorship, 109
Fitroy, A. T., 22
Flagellomania, 177–178, 182
Flaubert, Gustave, 124, 148
Fleurs du Mal, 148–150
Forster, E. M., 160
Fortune Press, 180
France, 34, 137–162
Freethinker, 101
Freud, Sigmund, 72–73

Friede, Donald S., 124
From Man to Man, 124
Fruits of Philosophy, 115, 123, 141

Garçonne, La, 159
Generative System, 166
Genius, The, 125
Germany, 181–182
Geschlechtsleben, 181
Gibbon, Edward, 14
Gide, André, 124
Gill, Eric, 126
Gilles de Rais, 169
Glass, Douglas, 75–82
Godwin, William, 71
Goncourt, de, 147, 154
Grand Guignol, 156
Grapes of Wrath, 133
Graphitae, cloacal, 176
Greek Anthology, 70
Greeks, 87, 185
Griffin, Frank, 155
Grose's *Classical Dictionary of the Vulgar Tongue*, 167

Hall, Sir Charles, 58, 91
Hall, Radclyffe (*see under Well of Loneliness*)
Hampstead Public Library, 106
Hanley, James, 102
Hard-Boiled Virgin, 124
Harvard University, 125
Heine, Maurice, 175
Hemingway, Ernest, 124
Henry VIII, 17
Heptameron, 146
Hicklin's case, 10, 40–41, 141
Himes, Norman E., 131
Hinton, James, 50
Hirschfeld, Magnus, 182

Hobbes, Thomas, 14
Homer, 128
Homosexuality, 87, 175, 177
Hotton, James Camden, 178
House of Commons, 67–68, 73, 101
Housman, Laurence, 92
How to Achieve Sex Happiness in Marriage, 132
Hugo, Victor, 14, 149, 154
Humour, 184–186, 187
Hunger and Love, 97
Huxley, Aldous, 70, 92, 174
Huxley, Thomas Henry, 46, 63
Huysmans, Joris Karl, 54, 153, 159

I Joined the Army, 155
Im Westen nichts Neues, 133
Index Librorum Expurgatorius, 14
Index Librorum Prohibitorum, 14–15
Indictments Act, 1915, 88–89
Indiscreet Confessions of a Nice Girl, 113
Industrial Revolution, 161
Ingram, Kenneth, 87
Insurance, 107–108
International Conference for the Suppression of Obscene Publications, 89, 141
Irish Catholic, 16

Janet March, 97
Jessel, Sir George, 91
John of Gaunt, 13
Joyce, James (*see under Ulysses*)
Judiciary, attitude of, 73, 83–86, 91, 93, 95, 127, 148, 149, 158, 160
Jury, trial by, 67, 82–85, 138–139

Index

Kanga Creek, 51
Keyserling, Count, 124
Kistemaeckers, Henri, 154–155
Knowlton, Charles (see under Fruits of Philosophy)

La Fontaine, 14, 152, 167
Labour Party, 73, 101
Laclos, Choderlos de, 147
Lady Chatterley's Lover, 125, 182
Lambert, R. S., 109
Lamp of Destiny, 86–88, 91
Lancret, Nicholas, 143
Larousse's Dictionnaire, 14
Laud, Archbishop, 18
Law—
  important cases—
    Sedley's case (1663), 18–20
    R. v. Dean of St. Asaph (1784), 22
    Phillimore v. Machin (1876), 16
    U.S. v. Certain Magazines (Marriage Hygiene), (1938), 131
    New South Wales v. Butterworth & Co. (1940) 17
    (See also under Bedborough, Bradlaugh, Curll, Hicklin, Montalk, Read, Ulysses: Appendix I of my The Banned Books of England for legal nomenclature)
  reporting, 157
Lawrence, D. H., 69, 125, 182
League of Nations, 61

Lees, Edith, 55–56, 61
Legitimation League, 58
Lewis, Sinclair, 124
Liberalism, 15, 38, 70–72, 95–96, 161, 190
Libraries—
  public, 103–107
  L.C.C. education, 101
  National Central, 104
  scholastic (see under Advocates, Bibliothèque Nationale, Bodleian, Boston Athenaeum, British Museum, Congress, London, Vatican)
  subscription, 100
Limericks, 186
Lisieux, Isidore, 180
Listener, 99, 109
Little Essays of Love and Virtue, 61
Locke, John, 14
Loi sur la liberté de la presse and amendments, 138–145, 153–156
London Library, 167
Long Parliament, 18
Lordly Lovesongs, 84
Louis XVI, 100
Louÿs, Pierre, 159
Lucian, 158

Madame Bovary, 148
Magistrates (see under Summary Jurisdiction)
Malthusian League, 140–141
Man and Woman, 57
Mansfield, Lord, 22
Mantegazza, Paolo, 134

201

Margueritte, Victor, 159
Marlowe, Christopher, 53, 152
Marriage Hygiene, 131
Marryat, Captain Frederick, 122
Martial, 158
Massingham, Henry, 59
Masturbation, 166
Meagher, F. W., 166
Meibomius, J. H., 29, 30, 35
Mencken, H. L., 62
Mermaid Series, 53–54
Michelanglo, 126
Middle Ages, 13, 185, 189
Mill, J. S., 14, 50
Millar, Henry, 70
Milnes, R. Monckton (later Lord Houghton), 175
Milton, 18
Mirabeau, 147, 150
Moll, Albert, 134
Monsieur Vénus, 153
Montagu, Ivor, 109
Montaigne, 14
Montalk, Count Potocki of, 75–96
Montifaud, Marc de, 152
Moore, George, 173
Moral theology, Latin works on, 39
Mouton, Mon. le Conseiller, 142
Murray, Gilbert, 185
My Life by Havelock Ellis, 59

Napoleon I, 145, 146
Napoleon III, 147
Nash, A. S., 132
National Council for Civil Liberties, 11

National Council on Freedom from Censorship, 11, 133
New Morality, The, 107
New Spirit, 55
New Statesman and Nation, 113
New York Book of the Month Club, 133
New York Society for the Suppression of Vice, 123
Newman, Frances, 124
Newsom, G. E., 107
Nineteenth century, 37–43, 122–123, 146, 161, 180
Novels, 69, 155, 159–160
Noyes, Alfred, 15
Nudist, 99
Nudist literature, 99–100
Nun in her Smock, 30, 32, 35

Obscene Literature in Law and Practice, 179
Obscene Publications Act, 1857, 39
Oil, 124, 133
Origin of Species, 66
Other Half, The, 110–111
Outrage à la morale publique et religieuse, 146–153
Outrage aux mœurs, 138–145, 153–157
Outrages publics à la pudeur, 138

Palace of Pleasure, 17
Pamela, 14
Pansies, 69
Pascal, 14
Pathologie des Emotions, 60
Paul IV, 126
Payne, John, 167–168

Index

Periodicals, 98–99, 139, 147, 155–156, 174
Perogative, royal, 16–18
Petronius, 126, 158, 180
Pictorial "obscenity," 99–100, 128, 178, 181
Picture Post, 16
Pillory, 32–33
Piron, Alexis, 147
Pius IX, 16
Poiteau, Mon. le, 143
Police Courts (*see under* Summary Jurisdiction)
Police evidence, 90
Political Censorship of Films, 109
Politics and moral censorship, 34, 133, 161
Pompadour, Madame de, 100, 146
Pope, Alexander, 25, 26, 27, 33
Pornography, 163–190
Postal authorities, 134–135, 188
Potocki, Count (*see* Montalk, Count Potocki of)
Pound, Ezra, 49, 70
Poulet-Malassis, 150
Power, 124
Press, 22, 110–115, 164
Prevost, l'Abbé, 146
Price of books, 101–102, 144, 149, 180
Priestley, J. B., 92
Printers, 98
Printing, invention of, 13
Prison life, 81–82, 93–94
Prisoner's Advocate, 31
Private publication, 167, 179, 188, 189
Prostitution, 115–119, 168

Proust, Marcel, 159
Public Morality Council, 113, 119
Publication abroad, 97
Publishers, 25, 97, 111–115, 150, 180
Pucelle d'Orléans, 146
Psychology of Sex, 61

Rabelais, 46, 78, 80, 126
Rachilde, Madame, 153
Rainbow, 69
Ranke, 14
Read's case, 23, 30, 34
Reformation, 16–17
Reigen, 124
Remarque, Erich Maria, 133
Renaissance, 17–18, 189
Restoration, 18–19
Rétif de la Bretonne, 145
Richardson, Samuel, 14
Richepin, Jean, 151
Right Review, 76
Robertson, John, 166
Robespierre, 146
Robie, W. F., 132
Rock Pool, The, 97
Romantic Movement, 159
Ronsard, Pierre de, 147
Roque, Jules, 156
Rousseau, 126
Routledge, Messrs. George, & Sons, 111–115
Royal College of Physicians, 62
Russell, Bertrand, 107, 124
Rutger, Johannes, 126

Sacrifice to Attis, 101
Sade, The Marquis de, 145, 174–176, 179

203

St. Pancras Public Library, 104
Sainte-Beuve, Charles Augustin, 148
Sand, Georges, 14
Sandbach, J. B., 99
Sanger, Margaret, 131
Sanger, William W., 168
Savoy, 57
Schnitzler, Arthur, 123, 124
Schreiner, Olive, 52–53, 124
Science, 69, 147, 158
Scotland, 41–42, 167
Scott, George Ryley, 127
Scott, Sir Walter, 36–37
Seditious libel, 22, 36
Sedley, Sir Charles, 18–21, 23
Sedley, Katherine, 20–21
Sewell, George, 29
Sex education, 103, 171, 175–176
Sex-morality Tomorrow, 87
Sexual Impulse, 69, 91, 165
Sexual Inversion, 57–60
Sexual Life in Its Biological Significance, 126
Sexualleben unserer Zeit, Das, 181
Shakespeare, 17, 19, 75, 128
Shaw, George Bernard, 50, 52, 71, 109
Shelley, 71
Si le Grain ne Meurt, 124
Sinclair, Upton, 124, 133
Sister Carrie, 97
Sistine Chapel, 126
Snobbery with Violence, 93
Sonnets by Havelock Ellis, 49–50
Sous-offs, 155
South, Dr. Robert, 28

Spectator, 55, 113, 160, 174–175
Stage censorship, 109
Star Chamber, 17, 18
Steinbeck, John, 133
Stendhal, 14
Stephen, Sir James, 42
Stopes, Marie Carmichael, 103
Story of an African Farm, 52
Strange but True Relation how Mr. Edmund Curll, etc., 26
Student Christian Movement, 132
Studies in the Psychology of Sex, 47–49, 57–61, 65, 66, 121
Sue, Eugène, 150
Suetonius, 169
Summary Jurisdiction, 67, 68, 69, 115, 117, 118, 138–139, 146, 155
Sumner, John S., 123–130
Sun Also Rises, The, 124
Sunday Express, 110
Surprising Songs, 77, 84
Swift, Jonathan, 38
Swinburne, A. C., 49, 54, 174, 175
Syllabus of Pius IX, 1869, 16
Symonds, John Addington, 53, 54, 57, 58
Symons, Arthur, 54, 56

Taine, 14
Tariff Act, 1930, 126, 131–132
Tarnowski, Benjamin Michael, 134
Taste, literary, 36–39, 93, 128–129, 173
Tentation de Saint-Antoine, 124
Thackeray, 37, 38
Thornton, Henry and Freida, 132

Index

"Thrillers," 173, 176
Time and Tide, 113
Times, 65, 88
Times Literary Supplement, 66
To Beg I Am Ashamed, 110–120
Towards Democracy, 53
Translations, 69–70, 72, 134, 158–159, 167–168, 181
Traumdeutung, Die, 73
Tropic of Cancer, 70
Tropic of Capricorn, 70
Twentieth century, 67–74, 123–133, 156–158, 180
Twilight, 124

Ulysses, 70, 81, 93, 127, 159
Universities, 62, 133

Vanguard Press, 127
Vatican Library, 145
Vénus dans le Cloître, 30, 32, 35
Verlaine, Paul, 54, 79, 150
Villon, François, 145, 183
Vizetelly, Henry, 53–54, 150
Vocabulary, 75, 78, 81, 85, 93, 117, 127–129, 182–184
Voltaire, 14, 15, 126, 146
Volterra, Daniele da, 126

Walpole, Sir Hugh, 92
Walpole, Robert, 29, 31
Warren, M. A., 123
Watteau, Jean, 143
Wayward Man, The, 124
Well of Loneliness, The, 90, 110, 159
Wells, H. G., 15–16, 50, 71–72, 92, 124
What I Believe, 124
Whited Sepulchres, 79–80, 94
Whitgift, Archbishop, 17
Whitman, Walt, 53
Wild, Sir Ernest, 82–91, 93
Wild Oats, 84
Wilde, Oscar, 57
Wolstonecraft, Mary, 71
Wood, Anthony à, 19
Woolsey, Judge, 127
Worby, John, 110
World I Never Made, 127
World of William Clissold, 124
Wyclif, 13

Yeats, W. B., 91

Zola, 150, 154